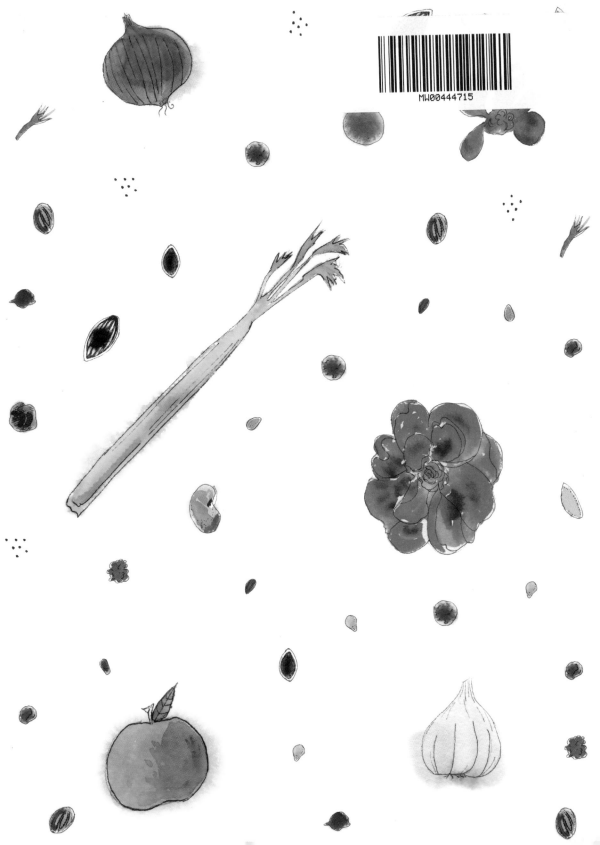

Drawn to
the Garden

To Rose and Will, the best things I've ever grown.

Quarto

First published in 2024 by Frances Lincoln,
an imprint of The Quarto Group.
One Triptych Place, London, SE1 9SH,
United Kingdom
T (0)20 7700 9000
www.Quarto.com

A catalogue record for this book is available from the British Library.

ISBN 978-0-7112-9055-6
Ebook ISBN 978-0-7112-9056-3
Audiobook ISBN 978-0-7112-9803-3

10 9 8 7 6 5 4 3 2 1

Publisher Philip Cooper
Senior Editor Laura Bulbeck
Design Sarah Pyke
Art Direction Paileen Currie and Isabel Eeles
Junior Designer Daisy Woods
Production Controller Eliza Walsh

Printed in Slovenia

Drawn to the Garden

Caroline Quentin

FRANCES LINCOLN

Contents

Preface

Once upon a time, long ago, a little girl lived with her mother. Sometimes her mother was unwell and went away to stay in a big dark house on a hill.

When her mother was away the little girl was sad and afraid. She felt ashamed of her mother's sickness and ashamed of feeling ashamed. She buried the sadness and the shame, deep inside like a hard, sharp seed.

One day, when her mother had been away for a long time, the little girl went into her garden and hid under an old apple tree. There, curled up in a tangle of weeds, she wept.

Then the sun came out. It dried her tears.

The little seed of sadness and shame was no longer hard and sharp. Watered by her tears, warmed by the sun and the soil, a tiny green shoot was emerging. One day the seed would blossom. This book is the result.

A growing passion

'*Ever tried. Ever failed. No matter.*
Try again. Fail again. Fail better.'

SAMUEL BECKETT (1906–89)

I've grown things, on windowsills, on balconies in planters and in increasingly large gardens for most of my life. I do it because it makes me giddy with happiness. In gardening, I have found comfort in my own company and camaraderie in the gardening community. If you're new to gardens and gardening you will be amazed at how easy it is to find a language and a means of communication with others that grow things. It's like speaking a universal language, like arriving in a foreign country and discovering that you can converse with the natives with ease, that somehow, even though you didn't know it, you share a common tongue and that the people of this land understand you, and you them. That they are welcoming and excited to share their ideas and customs with you. Wherever you go in the world, whether it be Barnsley or Bangkok, you will have 'family' there to greet you if you speak 'horticulture'.

Here in Devon, I garden with music, in silence, clothed or naked, on golden sunny days and by silvery moonlight. I garden alone and with company. I garden when I'm happy and when I'm sad. When I'm feeling good about life, gardening is a simple pleasure: planning, planting, harvesting and cooking. When my mood is low, it's a meditative and restorative pastime.

The act of doing something, that *by its very nature* is looking to the future, is good for me. I can focus on the present, sowing a tomato seed in a little compost, while looking forward with some hope because I know that very soon, if I'm lucky, a tiny green shoot will appear.

Gardening is the perfect antidote to my full-time job as an actor. Happily, theatre, TV and radio still interfere with my gardening life on a regular basis. Filming for TV usually happens in the summer because here in the UK the days are longer, lighter and better for location shoots . . . just as they are for green shoots. After the long, cold, dark winter months, as spring arrives, I'm always painfully aware, as I open up my greenhouse and potting shed for the new season, washing pots, cleaning tools and excitedly shuffling new, brightly coloured seed

packets from one hand to the other, that as soon as I'm absolutely ready to start sowing . . . the phone will ring. Like all actors since the dawn of time, I'm thrilled at being offered a job – my ego and my bank balance will be given a boost and I'm grateful that people still want to see me do what I've been doing for nearly 50 years.

Why then do I feel, increasingly, that the excitement and anticipation is tinged with a sense of reluctance? It's because, I think, I know that my time in the greenhouse, the garden and the potting shed will be seriously curtailed by my juvenile desire to show off, either on stage or in front of a camera.

I still get the same buzz planting out a courgette, that I had from growing parsley on a windowsill when I was 20.

As the years go by, I am finally realising that my time is precious and that I must make better choices as to how I spend this dwindling resource. I love being an actor but there has always been another, secret love, hiding just out of sight . . . a deep love for my garden. My two great passions have always had to compete for my time and attention but age and perhaps, finally, a modicum of maturity mean that I'm choosing to spend less time with that glittery, fickle, showbiz companion and opting to hang out with the calmer, kinder, more constant and reliable friend, my garden.

Those of you who follow my Instagram account @cqgardens will know that, much as I love my garden, I try not to be too earnest and worthy about it. When, many years ago, I first started to grow things, I often felt rather over-awed by television and radio gardeners, the experts in the field, if you'll pardon the pun. Sometimes they made gardening seem too daunting and difficult for a beginner, that it was something that could only be done by old men in roll-neck sweaters, who'd been to horticultural college and learned the dark arts of double digging and how to wrangle their hair into the perfect side parting.

They used a secret language – mulching and composting, leaf mould and potato blight, pinching out and tying in. I just wanted to grow basil on a window ledge. I didn't even have a balcony back then, so I was pretty sure that knowing how to dig a potato trench wasn't going to be particularly useful to me.

Years later I have come to realise that gardening, just like life, is a series of well-meaning cock-ups and happy accidents, unplanned successes and baffling and frustrating failures. Happily, unlike life, gardening mistakes are rarely worth crying about. I did lose an azalea to frost damage in the 1990s but I can talk about it now without sobbing – just. Generally, though, gardening is a low-risk hobby. Nobody gets hurt. As I write this though, I'm reminded of the time that I stood on a heavy garden rake (the metal end) and the long handle flipped up very quickly and with great force. I was hit hard, full in the face. It was a cartoon moment made real. Buster Keaton couldn't have played it better. Unlike the movies though, it really hurt and, unlike the silent movies, I let out an ear-splitting yelp and a string of expletives that Gordon Ramsey would be proud of. I thought I'd broken my cheekbone. It must have looked funny though because my husband was helpless with laughter – he couldn't contain his guffaws as he lovingly held an ice pack to my throbbing face. He's sitting next to me now and I've just reminded him of the event – annoyingly he's still trying to hide a smirk.

I love gardening because, unlike the rest of my life, a lack of knowledge, foresight and education don't hold me back. Nothing seems to dampen my enthusiasm; I still get the same buzz planting out a courgette, that I had from growing parsley on a windowsill when I was 20. When we grow plants, every day brings a small miracle.

I hope this book will encourage the novice gardener, the experienced gardener and even the non-gardener to fall in love with gardening in a whole new way. What I really want this book to do, is help silence the inner critic in us all, that nagging voice that tells us that our endeavours are not good enough, that there is no point in trying because our efforts are doomed to failure because we aren't up to it. Perhaps the most valuable thing that gardening can teach us is to forgive ourselves our failures and to celebrate our successes, however tiny, whether it's the green frilly triumph of a homegrown lettuce or spitting in the eye of a blighty potato – it should all be fun.

I've been lucky enough to be given the opportunity to provide the illustrations for this book, rather than having a professional artist put pictures to my words. Just as with my gardening exploits, some of my illustrative endeavours are more successful than others. That said, I have loved doing the pictures in this book. The hours spent leaning over the watercolour pad, pencil or paintbrush in hand, have been some of the happiest I've ever had. They have helped me rediscover the quiet delight of peaceful concentration that I had as a child, just colouring in, wax crayon in my chubby, sticky little fist. These mixed offerings have been done with love and in the full and certain knowledge that, just as I am an amateur gardener and an inexperienced writer, it's become clear to me that I am a novice illustrator.

I really hope that my hit-and-miss attempts at all three disciplines will encourage other would-be artists, writers and gardeners to pick up a pencil, a trowel or an idea and run with it. Give it a go. Being new to something is not a crime. We will make mistakes, people may think we are foolish, particularly if we are not young anymore, but it's a shame not to try something because we fear ridicule or because that nagging inner voice is stopping us. Learning something new is often scary and challenging but laughing at ourselves and our poor first attempts is a healthy response. Let's be proud of tiny steps forward and miniscule successes.

Let's give ourselves permission to mess up, go wrong, make mistakes and carry on. Shall we turn down the volume on our inner critic, get dirt under our fingernails, paint on our cardigans and put a big smile on our faces? Hell, why not, we've nothing to lose and so much to gain.

CHAPTER 1

Seeds

'I think that every seed is a miracle.'

CAROLINE QUENTIN

This tiny black speck is why I love gardening. It's not a mouse dropping or an apostrophe that's lost its way, it's a lettuce seed. Its only job is to grow. Given a little water, light, food and warmth it will get bigger and feed me. It will be delicious.

I think that every seed is a miracle. Seeds don't judge us. They don't care what dress size we are, what TV we watch or how we vote. They will, in return for a little attention, give us their best regardless of our race, gender, sexual orientation or star sign. Unlike children, puppies and other young things we might care for, seedlings won't wee on the carpet or sulk if we don't let them go out on a school night.

I was bitten . . . by the gardening bug and, like the bite of a midge on a Scottish holiday, I'm still scratching the itch.

In a world where our identity is constantly scrutinised, monetised and assessed, it's such a relief to know that whoever we are, we can be gardeners.

Even if you don't have a garden, if you have access to light, a little warmth and a drop of water, you can grow a seed. One of my earliest memories is of my first days at primary school, sprinkling tiny black cress seeds onto a damp piece of pink blotting paper. When you are five, life moves so slowly that by the time the cress had germinated a whole week later, I had completely forgotten the existence of the class project. When we were shown the results of our seed sowing, I was overwhelmed, shocked, thrilled. It seemed to me that where there had been nothing, there was now a forest of tiny pale trees with a dark green canopy. I was bitten, in that moment, by the gardening bug and, like the bite of a midge on a Scottish holiday, I'm still scratching the itch.

The following year our class progressed to bigger things and substantially bigger seeds. Runner beans – shiny, plump pink-and-brown speckled beauties, so smooth in our little hands. We put them in jam jars; again pink blotting paper was a part of the process. Funnily enough, I don't

recall using blotting paper since for propagating, but then I don't suppose
anyone under 50 would recognise a sheet of blotting paper. Ah, how
I miss a fountain pen – the horrible mess, the ink-stained fingers and
the illegible scrawl, the desperate pressing of the blotting paper on the
blotchy pages, the ruler across my knuckles and the exasperated shout of:
'What a mess, do it again!' With the use
of computers and the demise of the ink
pen I suppose they've found new ways
to humiliate our children and sow seeds.

*How can these
dried-up, minute,
inconsequential
little things fill our
plates, our stomachs
and even our souls
with such joy?*

It is over 50 years since I slid that
runner bean seed into the jam jar but
I still recall the sense of wonder when,
having scrutinised my jar every day for
what seemed like eternity only to find
nothing had changed, one morning
I could see a tiny, pale-green shoot
sprouting from the wondrous, spotty bean seed … and then! A couple of
days later the almost translucent, hairy roots appeared, searching for water.

By the end of term there were rows of jam jars with skinny snakes
of green, searching for the sunlight in our little classroom. I have no
idea what became of all those seeds. I can only imagine that our teacher
had a freezer full of runner beans, and enough cress to keep her in egg
sandwiches for the whole of the summer holidays.

Grow what you like

I now grow a huge variety of vegetables but truthfully nothing much has
changed for me when it comes to starting new plants every spring. Only
nowadays I always grow the things I love to eat. This means cress has
less of a role to play in my life but I do still grow runner beans, because
my husband adores them and, despite having to wait for the ground to
warm up before they go out into the garden, they are relatively easy and
fairly productive.

So, if you are new to gardening you might be wondering how to start your horticultural journey. I know that it's a well-trodden (garden) path but I'm going to say what all the experts say and that is, to grow what you like to eat. I'd also say it's wise to start with things that germinate quickly. If, like me, you are impatient, then nothing dampens the spirits like a long wait for a shoot to appear. Every year my first sowings are always lettuce and radishes – they only take three to four days to turn up. I freely admit to having the immediate gratification response of a four-year-old. My thought process goes something like this. Open seed packet, sprinkle seeds, water them. Wait 10 minutes . . . . *Where are the radishes? . . . . Where are they? Come on, come on . . . !*

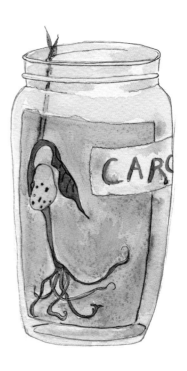

So my advice to you is, grow radishes, lettuce, spinach, marigolds, nasturtiums and cress as these are the first responders of the gardening year. When we desperately need them, after the long cold grey winter months, there they are, almost immediately, ready to help get us through the short, tough days of late winter and early spring, green and bright and full of joy and vitamins.

For a few quid or less, if you are lucky enough to be gifted or to have collected your own, you may have dozens or even hundreds of seeds. Even if a few duff ones fail to germinate you'll always get plenty of plants and very quickly have that heady rush of excitement and an unbecoming, overweening sense of pride at eating your very own homegrown produce. That said, some seeds are notoriously harder to germinate than others. These can include rosemary, asparagus, peppers and strawberries. I struggle with aubergines, always have, yet parsley germinates well for me even though others find it temperamental.

So, stick with the easy ones to start with and, as you get more confident or have more space or time, move on to the seeds that are a little more challenging.

How can these dried-up, minute, inconsequential little things fill our plates, our stomachs and even our souls with such joy?

Growing radishes

Here's how to grow a radish (or a few lettuce leaves). Get a small tray, with holes in the bottom, about the length and width of your hand and a few inches (7.5 cm) deep, something that had raspberries or blueberries in it perhaps – instead of recycling it, fill it with a layer of peat-free seed compost. Be sure to put it onto a tray or plate so that when you pour about a mug of water over it, it doesn't flood the work surface or tabletop and drench your electricity bill or knacker your mobile phone.

Open your chosen seed packet, follow the instructions on the back of the packet, pop the seeds onto the surface of the compost and cover in a light dusting of soil. Sprinkle with water and wait a few days, keeping the tray moist. I often cover it with a piece of clear plastic, to reduce evaporation and to warm the little darlings and get them going.

For those with a slightly scientific bent, it may interest you to know that seeds are high in carbohydrates, typically starch, which provide the energy for the little time bomb to germinate and send up a shoot. This will, as if by bloody magic, absorb sunlight, using chlorophyll, which is what makes plants green (all hail, mighty chlorophyll), and absorb carbon dioxide from the air and water through their roots. Once the seedling has sunlight, water and CO_2 it can start making its own food and so can *you*!

Basically, these tiny miracles take in greenhouse gases and give out oxygen. As if a plate of homegrown vegetables isn't glorious enough, vegetables are helping combat global warming, too.

This spring, why not give it a go? Before very long, you will have windowsills full of little pots of tomatoes, peppers, chillies, cucumbers and even, dare I say it, aubergines. Once you have experienced the joy of tasting something you've grown from seed, there is no going back.

Miracle grow

At this point I have to say that one of my obsessions is the difference in the colours, sizes and shapes of seeds. There are the tiny black full stops of mustard seeds, wrinkly beige spinach, smooth cream-and-red streaked borlotti beans, marigold seeds like weeny feathers, poppy seeds in their millions and almost invisible to the naked eye. They are all just a surprise waiting to happen. Delicate fennel seeds, which carry the same aniseed flavour as the bulb and its fine feathery fronds, simply don't look capable of producing the glorious, firm, deeply ridged, heavy bulb that will develop in just a few short weeks. The same size as an eyelash, this little parcel, once unwrapped, performs a transformation better than RuPaul in panto at the Palladium. And, once tasted, never forgotten.

I'm not sure that my love of seed sowing is just about the practical. It may sound peculiar to some and even completely whacky to others but for me, the act of popping a courgette seed (on its side is best, by the way) into a small pot and then covering it with a dusting of compost and a sprinkling of water, is a small meditation, a prayer – an act of intense hope and love. We are all trying to use less plastic, eat food that hasn't been flown halfway around the world, use less water, eat less meat, source our fish responsibly and generally give our poor, abused, achingly beautiful planet a fighting chance of survival. I often feel overwhelmed at the terrifying statistics about global warming, plastics in our oceans and the increasing poverty and starvation in the world but in the moment of sowing a seed, I feel part of a community of vegetable growers and eaters.

We are like seeds – apparently tiny and inconsequential but in reality, little powerhouses that, given some encouragement, can change things for the better.

If you already grow vegetables, you might be in the habit of collecting your own seeds. I'm rather late to this blindingly obvious practice. Perhaps because I'm susceptible to advertising or because I didn't come from a gardening family, I've only just realised that collecting seeds from my own plants is easy, cost effective and immensely satisfying. I'm not an expert but I really recommend giving it a go. With some plants it is so easy that it's rude not to!

A few flowers and vegetables will deliver their bounty freely and are simple to harvest (there are lots of others, of course, but because I'm new to this, I'll talk about the things I find easy). I imagine that once I become proficient, I'll do much more – perhaps we all will. I don't think we will put the seed companies out of business, because some vegetables are better grown from shop-bought F1 hybrids. What is an F1 hybrid? It is the result of crossing two different plants and creating a hybrid seed. This happens in nature anyway between species – peppermint, for instance, is a hybrid of water mint and spearmint. It's of little consequence to me that its parentage is so interesting, because my main obsession with it revolves around mint tea, mojitos and mint sauce. F1 hybrid seeds are more reliable and less likely to throw up genetic defects. This is handy for the novice gardener as it can smooth the path to the first tasty crop. That said, I feel it's really important to source heritage seeds and, when possible, to collect your own either from friends or from your own crops, or even from things you buy from the grocers. After all, diversity, happy accident and the unexpected are all part of the fun.

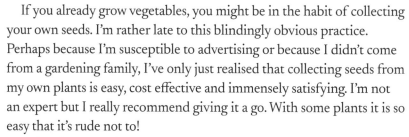

We are like seeds – apparently tiny and inconsequential but in reality, little powerhouses . . .

If you are going to give it a go, here are some seeds that are more straightforward to start collecting. I've grown from these methods, with some success, so why not give them a try? It's free and even if it doesn't work out, all you've wasted is a little time.

Self-pollinators such as beans and tomatoes are easiest as they always produce seedlings just like their parents. Some plants are much more likely to cross-pollinate and will produce different, sometimes unusual results so you're uncertain of what you might get. Although I'm happily a self-declared hit-and-miss gardener, there are some things I'd rather be sure of – I like to know that my onions and indeed my broccoli will be there for me in a form I recognise.

Tomato seeds

I'm starting with toms because I eat so many and, along with cucumbers, I probably grow more of these seeds than any other.

1   Use a teaspoon ... *Actually I use an odd little 1930s' Bakelite-handled butter knife that has been in the kitchen drawer, alone and palely loitering for as long as I can remember. I've no idea where it came from but I'm delighted it finally has a use, I digress ...* Most folk use a teaspoon. Scoop out the seeds from a tomato into a jar of water.
2   Soak them for two days. They will look like rancid frogspawn but don't give up on them. *Writing the word frogspawn, reminded me of my daughter who, when tiny, wrote up a nature experiment with the words 'look at the frogsporn'. I've never been able to erase from my mind the image of a hunky toad leaning back seductively on a lily pad, ready for red-hot amphibian love action. Anyway ...*
3   Using a tea strainer, rinse the jelly from the seeds.
4   Spread the rinsed seeds on kitchen paper and dry on a windowsill for a couple of weeks.
5   Store the paper with seeds attached. I usually pop mine in a brown paper bag and put them in a drawer until I need them.

6   Sow by laying the kitchen paper flat in a seed tray on a couple of inches (5 cm) of compost (it works like a seed tape) and water lightly, and grow on as usual.

Beans and peas

These really are easy ... PEAS(Y).

1   Let the pods develop fully on the plant and then leave a few nice chunky ones attached until they turn crisp and papery and beige. Keep an eye on the weather: try to gather them when the weather is fine, but if it's wet, cut a large section of the plant and hang it upside down in the greenhouse or in a light, warm room to finish ripening.

2   Pick the pods soon after they dry or they'll burst open unaided and scatter seed all over the place. *You'll be finding dried peas in unusual places for years to come. It's discombobulating to come across unexpected legumes in a laundry basket full of undies. Peas in your pants!* So, simply open the dried pods and store the peas or beans in a labelled envelope until the following spring.

Plants that form seedheads

These plants include lettuce, coriander and lots of others. I like the percussive element of collecting these seeds.

1   Let them flower and wait for the flower heads to go to seed and start to look dry and brittle. Cover smaller seedheads, like dill and coriander, with paper bags just as they're ripening. If you leave it too long they will disperse naturally and the seeds will fall on the ground before you have a chance to collect them.

2   Snip the whole head, still in the bag, from the stalk and turn it upside down and shake. *I love the sound! The tiny light seeds against the paper are like maracas in a fairy ASMR orchestra.* With a few

gentle shakes the seeds fall into the bag, ready to be stored and used next season. Some lettuce seedheads will need a bigger paper bag. I nick a few extra from the veg isle at my local supermarket – *there I said it* – or, failing that, I shake them into a bucket and decant into paper bags.

This is easy with poppy, aquilegia and lots of herb seeds, too. Just keep an eye on plants as they flower and gather dried seed heads. It's so satisfying to grow using home-gathered seeds.

Miss Willmott's ghost

While I'm talking about seeds, I must briefly mention Miss Ellen Ann Willmott, born in Heston, Middlesex (now greater London), in 1858. Her family were keen gardeners and Ellen grew up to be an influential horticulturalist, receiving the Victoria Medal of Honour from the RHS in 1897. A truly eminent plantswoman, she is thought to have had over 100,000 cultivars in her garden. Like many horticulturally frenzied, more commonly male, Victorian collectors (and thanks to huge inherited wealth), Ellen Willmott sponsored plant-finding expeditions throughout the world.

There are more than 60 plants bearing her name but thistle *Eryngium giganteum* is my favourite. Native to Western Asia and Iran, it's commonly known as Miss Willmott's Ghost. A truly spectacular, short-lived biennial species with a wonderful architectural shape, silvery green, maturing to a heavenly lilac blue, it's a real wow in the herbaceous border. Thistles are a good food source for insects and birds, of course, but the reason I love this one is because of the charming, funny and slightly anarchic story attached to it.

According to gardening mythology Ellen always carried pockets full of the tiny seeds and whenever she went to visit friend's gardens, and when no one was looking, she'd throw a handful into the borders, where they would germinate and come up unexpectedly, unplanned

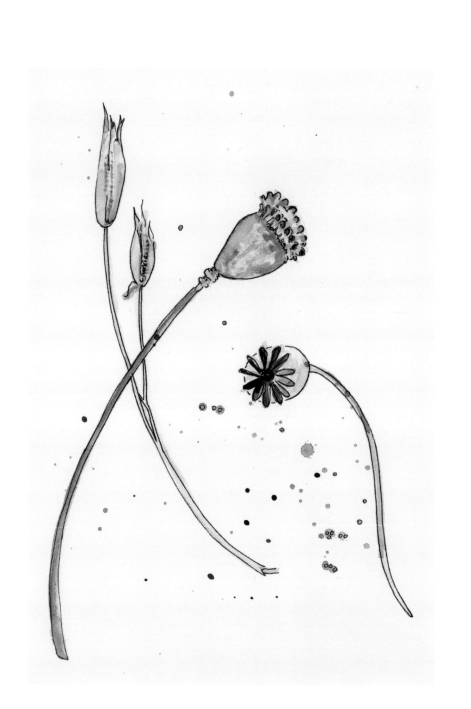

and unexplained the following season. I don't know or care if this story is true – I just love the idea of an outwardly respectable Victorian spinster surreptitiously doing her own thing. Ellen Willmott may have gone to the great garden in the sky in 1934 but her legacy is still seen in the glorious gardens of great houses. The stately figure of *Eryngium giganteum* silver, luminous in the herbaceous borders, is a ghostly reminder of the great plants woman. I urge you to chuck a few seeds into your patch of soil and think of Ellen. What a gal; what a ghost story.

Sweet peas

Once the flowers have gone over, the vines produce seed pods. When they are dry and are stiff and papery to the touch – be sure to do it before they spontaneously burst open and fire the seeds into the air – take the pods and split them carefully, putting the tiny cannon balls into a paper bag or envelope. Collect plenty as some might not germinate. You can start the seeds in the autumn if you have room on a windowsill or in the greenhouse.

CHAPTER 2

Memories

'One of the oddest things in life, I think,
is the things one remembers.'

AGATHA CHRISTIE (1890–1976)

I love that quote from Agatha Christie. I'm always amazed at the
memories that pop into my head: unbidden moments, unasked for
snapshots and seemingly useless technicoloured snippets of my
past, from the exact details of the fabric of my first party dress when
I was four years old to the feeling of bicycle tyres rolling over my ribs.
One sunny autumn day I'd hidden under a pile of leaves and a boy
called Darren (who knew I was there), deliberately cycled over me
(it didn't hurt but I recall exactly the sound and the smell of the
crunchy horse chestnut leaves).

I can recall events from 40 years ago with crystal clarity . . . playing
the Comedy Store for the first time, the chaos of the last dress rehearsal
before the opening night of the original production of *Les Miserables*
at London's Barbican theatre (I couldn't find my nun's habit for a quick
change on stage left and Jean Valjean had to wait). Yet when I try to
remember my own telephone number or what I was up to last weekend
my mind goes blank. Friends regale me with stories of what sound
like glorious parties at the Edinburgh Festival in the 1980s: days out,
weddings and all fun stuff that I really want to look back on, but not a
chance. It seems I am hard wired, like Agatha Christie, to recall only the
oddest of things.

Early memories (or, close encounters of the chrysanthemum kind)

One of my earliest memories of a garden, is from when I was about
three years old. I was just under 3 ft (1 m) tall when I came face-to-face
with a yellow flowerhead the size of a tambourine – I was very aware of
the size of a tambourine because I had played on one at nursery (rather
well, I like to think) only the week before. This first encounter with a
massive chrysanthemum bloom clearly made an impression on me. I
was in Avril's grandparents' garden. Avril was our lodger, a girl of about
18 who rented a room at the top of our tall semi-detached house in
Surrey. Avril's grandad grew chrysanthemums in the long thin garden

at the back of his caravan. I think I remember this because it was an unusual day for me, in lots of ways. I'd never met a grandparent before – mine had all died before I was born and Avril's grandparents made me wish I had at least one. Her grandparents were nice (think Raymond Briggs' *When the Wind Blows*). Also, I'd never been in a caravan before. I certainly had no idea that people lived in weeny little houses on wheels and I liked it a lot.

But without doubt, the stand-out moment for me was the garden, where the flowers grew taller than children! This was a revelation, a red letter day. (I think there may have been a slice of Battenburg involved, too, but my memory might be playing tricks, making a good day just too perfect.) The yellow of this (ball) chrysanthemum is seared into my memory, as though my personality was branded in that moment and that forever I would be in love with big bright flowers.

Chrysanths and dahlias have come in and out of fashion during my lifetime. Tastes change and, as with clothes, each generation likes to believe it is discovering something new, something that the previous generation simply don't 'get'. I may have tried to move with the times as far as garden planting goes but truthfully, I think when I was planting pale, delicate penstemons in the 1980s and an all-white border in the 90s, I was denying my true, gaudy, shouty, show-off inner plantswoman.

. . . forever I would be in love with big bright flowers.

Of course, there is room for everything in the garden and we all have our darlings when it comes to flowers. The crumpled-tissue petals of a lilac poppy or a potentilla are always welcome, but let me be honest here – what's not to love about a big, fat, bright pompom-headed chrysanthemum? OK they don't have a real scent to speak of, although in one of my favourite D.H. Lawrence short stories, 'The Odour of Chrysanthemums', Lawrence perfectly describes their unique smell: not pretty but stale, nostalgic and beautiful in a subtle, secretive way.

Perhaps that's why I love them. They are a bit like me. I appear a bit
brash and uber-confident, but like lots of us who seem to be extroverts,
we are in fact doing a very good job of covering up a quieter, more
reticent side of ourselves.

As an adult gardener I don't have to pretend to like things I don't
like, or to keep up with fashion, horticultural or otherwise. I have the
confidence to grow what I want, where I want. If that means dahlias
and chrysanthemums in a kaleidoscope of colour – with their great, big,
screaming, clashing, tasteless blooms that frankly should be ashamed of
themselves – then so be it. Sometimes it works and other times it all gets
a bit much. I don't care. Next year I'll try something else. It's my garden
and I can do what I want – as far as I know there are no gardening
police. Although those awaiting the judges at the Chelsea Flower Show
might disagree.

Future memories

I've just come in from the garden – tomorrow my friend's daughter is
getting married in our village church. I've offered my help with a few
floral bits and bobs. It's now 8 a.m. and I have been out since 6 a.m.
collecting flowers for tomorrow. Ellie, the bride, has asked if I could
provide some tiny flowers to add a bit of colour to the celebratory fizz.
I don't know much about edible flowers – I'm more of a ratatouille
woman myself and so, never having done this before, I'm keeping it
simple and only using flowers that I'm certain are edible and that I know
will look beautiful. I have collected some stems of flowering sage, borage
and some tiny rose petals, put them onto some damp kitchen paper
and popped them in the fridge until tomorrow morning when I'll have
time to separate the edible bits from the less tasty bits of the plants. I'll
take away any white/yellow bases of the rose petals as I know they can
be bitter and I will simply check the flowers from the sage for bugs and
spiders. I'll prepare the borage, which I've used before in Pimm's, by
using a pair of tweezers to pull out the centre of the flower – basically

the stamen and the sepals – so that I'm left with just the beautiful bright blue star of the borage flower (these are brilliant frozen in single cubes of ice as an addition to summer drinks). I'm also going to use petals from my very prolific nasturtiums – they will certainly provide fantastic flashes of colour to liven up the wedding party drinks.

BREAKING NEWS . . .

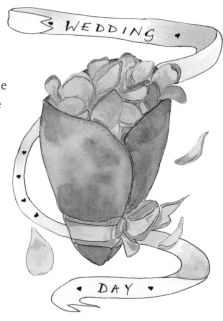

I've just had a rather worried phone call from the mother of the bride. The dried rose petals that have been ordered to be thrown as confetti as the happy couple leave the church have been delivered to the wrong address. My roses have done very well this year so I've said I can provide fresh rose petals as a sort of living confetti. I'm taking a break now to get into the garden and gather as many petals as I can and get them into the fridge overnight, ready for tomorrow's 3 p.m. service.

Done it. I've got baskets full of the sweetest smelling, most beautiful rose petals. All I need to do now is put a few handfuls into separate containers and hand them out to the congregation before the wedding service tomorrow. Hopefully Eleanor and Tom will leave the church in a shower of pink and pale-yellow petals. It's made me so happy to be able to put my garden to use in a totally different way and for such a romantic and hopeful event.

Marking special occasions

As I was gathering the rose petals, I was thinking about the way people often use plants to mark events. They are so often used ceremoniously in our lives, for weddings, parties and religious ceremonies of all kinds. I remember travelling in India many years ago and seeing sulphur-yellow marigolds floating down the river alongside a flaming funeral pyre, the golden blooms accompanying the deceased on their last journey, down Mother Ganges. The bright oranges and reds of the marigolds and roses floating down the murky waters of the river and the wailing of the mourners will stay with me forever.

What opening night is complete without a big bouquet of flowers?

What opening night is complete without a big bouquet of flowers? I recall seeing Lynn Seymour curtsying deeply as roses were showered onto the stage by an enthusiastic audience who had seen her dance *La Fille mal gardée* (or was it *Coppélia*?) – either way it really wouldn't have been the same without the beauty of the flowers.

Today plant breeders, particularly rose growers, have realised the importance of plants when it comes to commemorating important events in our lives. For weddings, roses are always a favourite gift – 'Wedding Day' and 'Lovely Bride' are good choices. There are plenty of smaller roses bred specifically as patio plants that are ideal for those with smaller plots. 'Newly Wed' is lovely patio rose.

For more sombre events, 'Loving Memory', 'Fond Memories' and 'Remember Me' are plants to mark the loss of someone important in one's life.

When my darling mum, Katie, died on 1 July, 2012, I planted several things to mark her life. Katie was a redhead so I created a long border with bright red *Cornus* 'Midwinter fire' to remind me of not just her glorious hair but of her sometimes fiery nature. The border also has a

Canadian bunchberry *Cornus canadensis*, as she was born in Montreal, Canada. There's a maple in pride of place and, not far from the border, is a small apple tree, 'Katy'. Utterly beautiful and early in the season, 'Katy' produces pounds of bright red fruits that are sweet and crisp. It's always the first apple to blossom and fruit in my garden and gives me a little nudge to take the time to think about my mum, who was also small and sweet. Even if you haven't a relative called Katy, I really recommend this tree. It doesn't take up much room and I have found it to be totally reliable and problem-free.

Mum is buried under a copper beech, which, as it becomes more majestic every year, helps me to cope with the sadness I still feel at her loss and reminds me of the cyclical nature of the natural world and the beauty and benevolence of Mother Earth.

For happier times, I always plant sweet peas 'Happy Birthday' and 'Sweet Caroline' and hope that with regular picking, feeding and watering I can keep them alive to continue to bloom up until my birthday on 11 July. Then I can have little vases of the gorgeous, highly scented flowers on the table for my annual celebratory lunch.

A rose by any other name

About 20 years ago, in a garden I had in Suffolk, just for fun, I planted a 'showbiz' border. I sought out plants named after singers, actors and variety turns. Sweet pea 'Cliff Richard' clambered over fuchsia 'Barbara Windsor'. An unlikely sight both in the garden and in the flesh, I fancy. The dark crimson rose, 'William Shakespeare', sat alongside sweet peas 'Romeo and Juliet' and rose 'Tess of the d'Urbervilles'. (Hardy's tragic heroine is deep red like the murdered Alec's blood, which seeps through the ceiling of the boarding house when poor Tess murders the vile man.) Dignified and upright, with perfect deportment, primula 'Margot Fonteyn', sat elegantly in a little terracotta pot casting a benign eye over the gorgeous rose 'Darcy Bussell' – both performed well I'm pleased to say. Gardening royalty were represented by sweet peas 'Monty Don' and 'Alan Titchmarsh' (just like their namesakes, both were easy on the eye and smelled divine).

Having a flower named after you is a real accolade and looking through old books and catalogues is like a wonderful who's who from times gone by. Who was Albertine? Zéphirine Drouhin? Sweet William? Claude Monet has a rose named after him – surely the iris and waterlily growers are missing a trick here? I can think of a few people who should have a cactus named after them but I rather fancy having a vegetable named after me... what about beetroot 'Quentin's Red Reliable' or potato 'Caroline's Big Cropper'?

There is something comforting ... in the thought of the wind rustling through the leaves of the tree you have planted in memory of a loved one ...

If you have room in your garden to plant a reminder of a friend or family member who you've lost I think it's a wonderful thing to do – it could be a small area, a place under a tree to sit quietly and think about them, or even a water feature, a wind chime or a terracotta pot with a rose or a scented shrub. If you don't have a garden or outdoor space, then there are wonderful charities, arboreta and memorial gardens – the Woodland Trust Life for a Life scheme, RSPB celebration trees, Reforest Britain, The National Forest – that will plant trees on your behalf.

There is something comforting (even when you are unable to visit), in the thought of the wind rustling through the leaves of the tree you have planted in memory of a loved one, or of a bench under a willow. They can be a place of comfort for someone who is dealing with loss or sadness – a place where birdsong and nature are the gentle soundtrack to grief, memories and perhaps a gradual acceptance of loss.

CHAPTER 3

Salad

'Growing salad, it's not rocket science,
unless you're growing arugula.'

CAROLINE QUENTIN

W hen I was growing up in 1960s' suburbia, salads were not as we know them today. My salad days consisted of limp lettuce leaves, half a tomato and a spring onion, all invariably drowned in 'salad cream' or a tinned concoction of diced potato, peas and carrots in a claggy vinegar emulsion. I think it was called 'Russian salad' but it looked like puke – perhaps the then ever-present Cold War inspired the naming of the horrid stuff.

Mercifully the introduction of colourful healthy vegetable crops from around the world has changed our culinary and gardening landscape forever. Salad is no longer a form of punishment on a hot day as it was in my youth but an opportunity to savour diverse and exciting flavours. Salad leaves are in themselves a cause for celebration, for the gardener, the home cook and even the amateur artist!

Salad is cheap, healthy and very easy to grow. It's a great starting place for the novice veg grower. They are quick to germinate. Requiring very little in the way of care, they are some of the crops we can all enjoy, whether we are cultivating in a huge plot or on a cramped window ledge.

If you sprinkle lettuce, rocket and mizuna (Japanese mustard greens) seeds onto a little moist compost and keep it damp and warm, in less time than it takes to get through to BT customer services you'll have a full-on, sexy-as-all-get-out bistro salad.

Do the same with basil, broccoli and coriander – keep them in the dark for a few days – and in a fortnight you'll be eating super-nutritious, incredibly trendy sprouted greens, which no modern chef worth their Michelin star can resist sprinkling on ... well ... *anything*. While eating out recently, I found basil seedlings on vanilla ice cream. I thought at first sight it might be a soupçon pretentious ... but hand on my heart, darlings, it was truly *delicieux*.

One of the reasons I recommend growing salad leaves to those at the start of their gardening journey, is that there are so many flavours available. There is sure to be at least one that you'll like. I know it sounds obvious but a bed full of mizuna is a literal waste of space if bitter peppery flavours aren't your thing. Here is a small selection of the salad leaves readily available as seeds. I've grouped them together so that if you are unfamiliar with the varieties, it may save you wasting time and money growing things that you'll never use.

Bitter leaves

These are for you if you like a bit of fire on your tongue and in your belly. There are many health claims made about eating bitter salad leaves. I have no medical knowledge, but it makes sense to me that they may be good for digestion and to stimulate the gut.

Chicory rossa

This is the diva of the salad leaves. It reminds me of Maria Callas dressed in magenta silk, her moon-pale skin glistening in the spotlight at La Scala, Milan. It deserves to be centre stage with its strong flavour, satisfying crunch and real va-va -voom! If salad can be sexy, it's this.

Mizuna

A Japanese green, these sharply serrated leaves, I think, add real style to a salad. If you are a bit wary of turning the heat up, it's a good introduction to a spicy note in the most ordinary salad. You can eat the flowers, too. Grown outside, it's hardy for many months. I grow it in a pot by the kitchen door. A handful wakes up a piece of grilled chicken or halloumi, like a cymbal crash wakes a snoozy major in the front row at Glyndebourne.

Watercress

This is *the* bitter leaf to grow, even if you haven't room to grow a beard. Add a little compost to an empty container, poke in some drainage holes (or rather drinking holes), sprinkle a few seeds, keep the bottom of said container submerged in water (a serving dish or baking tray works

a treat for this) and *Dorothy, we're in Oz*! Watch the little Emerald Forest come up. If you've room, do a few trays and join the food fashionistas, using the baby, early leaves as micro-greens. Then, if you keep it wet (the clue is definitely in the name), you've a supply of salad leaves *and* a mini medicine cabinet. Watercress is crammed with vitamins and minerals, calcium and vitamins C and E. It's a part of the nasturtium family, which brings me to . . .

Nasturtiums

I grow nasturtiums for so many reasons. They truly are the member of the cabbage family that just keeps on giving. They stop the bugs from bugging my dahlias by distracting them, their trailing habit softens the edges of the raised beds and the hard landscaping in the veg garden, the bees adore them, the colour they provide makes the dullest of days scream summer AND you can eat them. Use the peppery, soft baby leaves in a salad – I love their neat almost translucent, sea-glass-green circles. Then, as if they haven't done enough, the nasturtium gives us her flowers. Shake well, removing any little creatures, carefully separate the bright petals from the green cup of the sepals and, once you've made your salad, place a few of the velvety flowers on top of the green. Honestly, if you've never served nasturtium flowers, it will fill you with delight.

Mild but interesting

If you prefer a less bitter taste, these are delicious without being bland.

Lamb's lettuce

Supposedly called this because its leaves resemble a lamb's tongue; indeed, I can verify that, here in Devon where I live, when lambs open their mouths to bleat for their mothers, they reveal a chubby, elongated lobe-shaped tongue, although I've only ever seen pink ones, never green! Also known as corn salad, lamb's lettuce is simple to grow. The secret, as with lots of vegetables that are ready to pick in a few short weeks, is to sow a little and often. Succession sowing (sowing a new row regularly throughout the season) is a useful habit to develop – however, I'm so disorganised that I must put notes in my diary to remind me. Occasionally my entries are slightly confusing: *Tuesday 11 a.m. dentist, Book hygienist – 1 p.m. Pick up dry cleaning. 3 p.m. yoga in the village hall. Send card to Rachel, Beetroot, Radishes, Pricking out.*

Lettuce freckles
For sheer good looks I always grow freckles. You can be eating these within 28 days. It's a bright green romaine lettuce, splashed with crimson. It's proven to be very successful here in Devon. Well worth giving it a go.

Lollo rosso
This is a tender, crisp, sweet and nutty lettuce. For some reason it's always reminded me of Kate Bush in her 'Wuthering Heights' days. I think it's the magenta colouring and luscious curly nature of the lettuce head . . .

Spring onions
Once you've mastered lettuces, the next thing you could turn to for easy growing is the spring onion. In the USA they call them scallions or green onions.

Sow outdoors from March onwards in small batches every couple of weeks to give a continuous supply. They don't take up much room and they do well for container gardeners, too. Be aware, in damp weather, slugs and snails might be a problem. You can make early sowings in a greenhouse using the same methods as outdoor. There are so many varieties available. I love to grow a mix of red and white salad onions – the colour adds so much.

Little gem

This is an adorable little lettuce and has been a favourite for generations of gardeners for very good reason. It's got great flavour, is sweet and high in vitamins A, C and K, and it's also a very good source of potassium and calcium, iron and fibre. Use in the same way you'd use any romaine lettuce – I liven it up with a simple vinaigrette dressing:

- 2 tsp Dijon mustard
- 2 tbsp red wine vinegar
- 6 tbsp olive oil
- A pinch of brown sugar (optional)
- Salt and pepper (optional)

Stick all the ingredients in a clean jam jar and do your best 'Tom Cruise in the movie *Cocktail* impression' and you're ready to go.

Radishes

If you want to grow radishes – and why wouldn't you want to grow radishes?– buy a packet of seeds, and follow these instructions:

1. Scrape out a little drill (a shallow trench) in the soil, and drop in one radish seed.
2. Then, using your hand to space them, add in another. Continue until you have about 10 seeds in a row.
3. Cover them over with soil, then firm down using the same hand you used to measure with.
4. Water lightly, pop in a plant marker and in no time at all you'll be harvesting hot, bite-sized, pink, red or white delicious little roots.

Eat them either washed, as they are, or sliced in a salad. Or, as the French do, with a smidge of butter and then dipped in flaked salt. Gorgeous. A healthier snack to serve with drinks than the ubiquitous crisps and peanuts, radishes also look much prettier, I think.

Cucumbers

For some reason growing my first cucumber was one of the finest achievements in my gardening life. Watching a weeny pale-green baby, smaller than my little finger, swell and grow into a full-size cucumber the likes of which I'd only ever seen in a greengrocers was magical.

I always start my cucumbers indoors – they germinate very well and the baby plants require little looking after. If you are lucky enough to have a greenhouse, once they are in the soil, keep them moist every couple of weeks and give them a feed of something high in nitrogen. Don't overwater them – if the leaves go yellow and floppy, take off the weakest ones and reduce watering.

As far as I'm concerned, the very best way to eat a cucumber is to slice it with a mandolin, laying the slices in concentric circles, like translucent jade disks. Now drizzle a little olive oil, salt and pepper and decorate with either a bit of dill or a few borage flowers. I know it's simple but a homegrown cucumber freshly picked doesn't need a full production number, just a spotlight and a chance to shine.

Tomatoes

OK let's cut to the chase. If you like tomatoes and have never had the chance to grow your own, once you have tasted a warm, freshly picked tomato popped into your mouth from between your fingers – your fingers that are still scented by the tomato leaves – you haven't lived.

If you are limited for space in your greenhouse, should you have one, there are plenty of varieties that can be grown outside. Indoors, in warm conditions, they are easy to grow.

1   From late February to mid-March you can sow the seeds in small
     pots of seed compost, spreading three seeds on the surface. I cover
     mine with a mixture of vermiculite, which is a hydrated mineral
     that absorbs moisture. *It looks like cat litter, but, I think, gives seeds a
     good start.*
2   Cover with clear plastic and within about 14 days the tiny seedlings
     will appear.
3   Uncover them and get them into as much light as you can.
4   Two weeks later, move your seedlings into individual pots. Fill these
     pots with peat-free multipurpose compost, water well and, using an
     old pencil, a lolly stick or your finger, make a hole and, very gently,
     holding the seedling by a leaf, *not the stem*, lower it into the hole.
     If it's a bit spindly you can bury it up to the first pair of leaves.
5   Tuck it up in its new bed, water regularly and in a month's time you
     can put the little plants into their final home.
6   If they are going outside you'll need to harden them off by keeping
     them in a cold frame. Failing that, put them outside when it's warm
     but make sure you bring them in at night otherwise all your hard
     work will have been in vain. Don't
     let them dry out when it's hot – you might need to water regularly.
7   When the first little yellow starry flowers have arrived, feed
     with a tomato fertilizer as directed. It's a liquid feed and so
     easy to apply.

Pollination can be a bit hit and miss in a greenhouse so, if at all possible,
leave doors and windows open as bees are by far your best friends when
it comes to pollinating tomatoes and, apart from anything else, they are
just such good company. Otherwise, although I've never tried it, hand
pollination is apparently easy, either by tapping the back of the flower
head to release the pollen or I've heard of some people who use an
electric toothbrush, which, thinking about it, probably perfectly mimics
the buzzing of the bee.

Varieties

When it comes to choosing varieties, the world's your oyster. In the greenhouse I like to grow a selection of the things I know I'll use. This means I'll always grow a large, sweet Mediterranean-style tomato. RHS 'Tomande' is even better than a classic 'Marmande'. It's truly reliable and utterly delicious. Another favourite that I highly recommend is 'Black Krim' ('Noire de Crimée'). I get these seeds from Sarah Raven. It's a Russian tomato so understands the British weather and what's even more brilliant is that it's an indoor/outdoor variety.

I really recommend growing at least two sorts of cherry tomatoes, three if you've room – a yellow, a red and an orange – because a salad made up of these three colours with a generous tearing of fresh basil is a sight to behold. 'Sungold' is popular for very good reason – its long, weighty clusters are very reliable and the dark-tangerine colour is wonderful against the yellow of tomato 'Katie Bell F1'. Remove the side shoots from cordon varieties (grown as a single-stemmed vine), if not, let them run riot. If you can manage to vine-ripen them they will be even more delicious.

When it comes to red cherry tomatoes there are so many different varieties. For reliability and a massive yield, Gardener's Delight is still ... a delight, but part of the fun of tomato growing is seeking out your own favourites. Every year I try at least one new tomato but my problem is letting go of old favourites so I often end up with a tomato glut.

This is relatively easy to cope with where I live as I have room to preserve tomatoes in lots of different ways but I appreciate that 12 tonnes of ripe tomatoes in a bedsit or small flat might be problematic. So it's best to try and grow only what you can use or store sensibly. Having read that sentence back to myself I can see what a total tomato hypocrite I am. I have never once managed to stick to this rule myself. However, as I've always said to the children, 'do as I say, not as I do'. They ignore me too.

The feast

As with cucumbers I really believe that tomatoes are best served as simply as possible and as soon as possible after picking. A big bowl of mixed colours, shapes and sizes always looks vibrant and so tempting. I prefer a sloosh of olive oil, a pinch of sea salt and a grinding of black pepper – perhaps basil, perhaps not.

Some of the bigger tomatoes are glorious when cut in half and slammed cut-side down on a very hot griddle or BBQ.

If you get a few full, heavy tomato vines, cut them off at the stem and either roast them or griddle them in a hot frying pan, letting the skins catch just a little. This seems to bring out the sweetness and adds a new dimension to really simple dishes. An omelette with a roasted tomato vine is possibly my favourite supper of the summer.

If you really have overdone the sowing, as I always do, you can store tomatoes very simply by filling carrier bags with whole fruits exactly as they come off the plant. Put them straight into the freezer where they become as hard as billiard balls and are easy to turn into a soup or a passata when you've time. Frozen tomatoes will keep in the freezer for six months.

CHAPTER 4

Wellbeing

'To mis-quote Dorothy Parker: You can take to horticulture, it's cheaper than a shrink…'

CAROLINE QUENTIN

Good mental health, like good physical health, is not something that any of us can take for granted. My mother suffered from what we would now call bipolar disorder. Back in the 1960s it was called 'manic depression', the name accurately describing the two extremes of mood that come with the territory. For my mother this meant periods of extreme elation, creativity and sleeplessness followed by periods of brutal dark depression. As a small child life with my mum could feel uncertain and sometimes insecure.

During her manic episodes she would do some strange things. I recall, one Christmas term, getting home from school to be greeted by my mother, thrilled that she had completed the festive preparations, proudly showing me the fire grate piled high with glass baubles and tinsel and the Christmas tree decorated with screwed-up bits of newspaper.

There were days and nights full of creativity and spontaneity, sometimes her 'mania' was exhilarating to be around. Occasionally she'd come to pick me up from primary school wearing just a diaphanous night dress, always late, her bright red hair tangled and wild. She'd call my name and then scoop me up in her arms and cover me in warm, loving, lipsticky kisses. I was five and mortified with embarrassment, other mothers weren't like this in their sensible shoes and beige slacks.

The upside of an embarrassing mother was the pride I felt in my mother's talents. She could paint and draw and play the piano to an impressively high standard, she was witty and smart and the funniest person I've ever met.

With bipolar disorder, the ups do inevitably, like Sussex, come with the downs. My mother took several overdoses. I'm not sure if these were deliberate attempts to end her life and get off the exhausting rollercoaster of her mental illness or just the accidental doubling, trebling or quadrupling of lithium, valium and the myriad of other medication that she'd been prescribed. In the corner of the sitting room was a wooden desk, drawers full of glass brown bottles and handfuls of loose tablets. Reds, blues, greens, whites and yellows – a veritable rainbow of pharmaceuticals. If you were to use this colour palette for a planting scheme at Chelsea Flower Show I'm pretty sure you wouldn't win any medals.

Sometimes unable to function at all, mum would lie in bed, the floral curtains drawn, not speaking, barely moving. Not tranquil exactly, but almost certainly tranquillised. Night and day were all one to her when she was low. Then one morning, I'd peep around her bedroom door and she'd be gone, the bed empty. Help had been called and the psychiatrists had decided to take her back to the 'loony bin' as she always referred to it. Sometimes, for her own safety, she'd be in a locked ward and from time to time undergo electroconvulsive therapy (ECT). This is a psychiatric treatment, still used today, where muscular convulsions are electrically induced to manage mental disorders.

When mum was feeling better I was allowed to visit her, usually spending time in the hospital gardens. I have a photograph of myself, aged about eight, on a bright summer's day surrounded by Michaelmas daisies. I knew the big white flowers were called Michaelmas daisies because mum told me they were (I've since learned that they are actually Marguerites – but expecting a non-gardener on a cocktail of medication to know the correct horticultural nomenclature is probably unwise). In the photo I'm wearing a white ballet tunic and pink ballet shoes. I can only surmise that someone had taken me to visit 'the bin' before my ballet lesson. I look uncomfortable and shy but I suppose, at eight, that's normal. Even though the photograph is faded and nearly 60 years old, I can see by the expression on my face that I am happy to be where my mother is, however briefly. I still love Michaelmas daisies or Marguerites . . . or *Argyranthemum frutescens* as I like to call them.

Why am I telling you all this?

What has all this got to do with the perfectly lovely topic of
gardening? Well for me, mental health and nature are inextricably
linked. I genuinely believe that growing things, watching the birds,
smelling the roses, eating the green stuff and drawing and painting,
all help keep me this side of sanity and one step away from the big
dark house on the hill. Over the years, I have tried all of the usual
numbing agents to stop the sometimes overwhelming sadness/
happiness thing. They don't work for me. The natural world is my
go-to, the hand that I hold when I need comfort, my stability in an
unstable world.

   I know, too, from correspondence with lots of folk that for so
many of us, nature helps. It helps to heal the sore bits of our psyche,
whether that be the old wounds of childhood or the more recent
cuts and bruises of day-to-day living in what can be a tough, lonely
and isolating world. As I get older, I realise that so many people
who appear to be just fine and dandy on the outside are sometimes
presenting a facade that is hiding a cracked and crumbling interior.
In my own life I know I have so much to be grateful for, please
believe me when I say that I'm aware of how ridiculously lucky I am.

*The natural
world is my
go-to . . .*

For what it's worth, I don't believe we 'make our
own luck', some of us are just more fortunate than
others. We are born in the right place at the right
time, have good people in our lives, enjoy good
health and are generally 'jammy sods'.

   I'm delighted to tell you that my mum's mental
health improved as the years went by. She lived happily into her
eighties with a bad tempered cat and an over-entitled Maltese terrier
and, despite loving flowers, she never could tell her asters from
her hellebores.

Small meditations in and connected to nature
(for those who don't really meditate)

I wonder how many of us recall the close-up examination of nature that, as children, we took for granted? Recently I saw my friend's little boy lying on his belly, his face a few centimetres (or inches as I still like to think of them) away from a spider's web. He was totally absorbed in the grizzly examination of a spider wrapping a fly in its silky web, like a ready meal in clingfilm. The child was entirely focused on what he was observing – watching a spider preparing to devour its prey was all he needed in that moment. He wasn't thinking about computers or television, food or even people.
He was satisfied, calm and peaceful.

I can vividly recall, as a child, staring at a daisy for minutes at a time, looking so closely at its little sunny face that I'd have a dusting of yellow pollen on my nose. The gold of its centre was mesmerising, and youthful eyes meant I could see its stamen, stigma and anthers without reading glasses. The tiny white petals observed so closely revealed a pearlescent magic sheen. It was an entire world on a slender stem.

One autumn I put a piece of fungus in a matchbox and kept it there for months. I loved taking it out and scrutinising its subtle striations of colour. Unfortunately, I discovered, if you keep a piece of fungus in a matchbox for too long it shrivels up to a piece of dried leathery nothing and someone chucks it in the dustbin while you are at Girls Brigade.

I believe as adults we can learn from our childhood selves and regain the peace that comes from closely observing nature. It might work for you, if ever you need a moment of respite from troubling thoughts.

Try some of these.

Find something from the natural world to look at

This might be a flower, a leaf, a spider's web, or if you simply can't access the outdoors, an apple or a carrot will do! Hold whatever you have chosen to give your full attention to, close enough to your face so that you can really see and even smell it. Find a good source of light. The sun is excellent, daylight is good however cloudy the skies, but a good lamp will suffice.

Now *look* at it. Soak up as much information as you possibly can. Give in to the meditative moment of bliss. I like a big blousy dahlia or tulip or rose but a fresh green leaf can be equally fascinating, *if* you give it enough time and attention. The colour palette will be very different for a leaf, of course, but sometimes the greens, browns and greys are as lovely as the brighter colours. Look at the colour. If it's red, ask what sort of red is it? Pillar box, maybe scarlet?

Perhaps it's pink, but what sort of pink? Gentle candyfloss pink or shouty fluorescent Barbie pink. Does the colour change as the petals near the centre of the bloom? What happens where the petals meet the stem? What's inside? Open up the flower head – what's in there? A tight group of pollen-laden stamen? A little black bug? I like to imagine I'm a bee looking for pollen at this point, but I do understand I'm a bit peculiar and that less eccentric people are happy to forgo this part of the process! Now *very* slowly turn the bloom in your hand. You've seen what's on show, but have you looked at the reverse? You can take my word for it that what's going on backstage is often much more interesting than the show itself!

Try to love the imperfections that are revealed. If the flower is beginning to wither and die, observe the gentle fading of colour, the wrinkling of the once perfect petals becoming even more fragile and the scent changing from a robust perfume to a more complex scent of decay. Value the imperfections. This is sometimes hard to do in a world where only perfection is deemed to have worth, where to be good looking in a conventional way is so prized and aging is seen as a sort of failure to be altered, as though the inevitable decline of living things should be ignored or is in some way shameful and ugly.

Examine your flower or your leaf, the fresh bits, the perfect bits and the imperfect bits.

It's all beautiful, it's all important and it all deserves our attention.

A breath of fresh air

If you can get out into the open air, I find a few deep breaths can change my mindset. It's better still if you can take off your shoes and socks and feel the earth beneath your feet. Obviously if you're in a park where people exercise their dogs, keep the shoes and socks on!

1   Breathe in deeply through your nose for at least three seconds and hold it in for a further two seconds.
2   Next, exhale for at least four seconds through the mouth.
3   You can repeat this exercise a couple of times.
4   Gradually transition into natural breathing.

A big green hug

When I have time, I try to get into the woods. Even if it's only for an hour or two. Some of my best conversations are with trees. I appreciate their lack of opinions and the way they simply refuse to give me any advice. So often when I'm struggling to make sense of a situation, a relationship or a decision, well-meaning friends offer solutions, but a copper beech keeps its own council. An oak tree just looks down, silently, and gives me permission to 'be'. Trees are never too busy to hang out with me, they always seem to make time, and unlike other friends over the years, they are always exactly where I last saw them. Of course, storms or old age occasionally take a tree's life, but generally they live longer than animals – a Scots pine can live for up to 500 years, an oak up to 1,000 – so we really can count on them to be there for us longterm.

Forest bathing

The Japanese practice of *shinrin-yoku*, or forest bathing, differs from a walk in the woods because it's not about the act of striding out and moving through the trees at pace, it's about connecting with nature using all the senses.

Walk slowly, look around, look up, look down. Look at the leaves, the tree canopy, the fungi, the insects; listen to the birds, the buzz of the insects, the trees and grasses rustling; smell the pine, the bark, the dampness of the earth or the heat of the day; taste the clean air as you fill your lungs and breathe deeply.

Try to accept the kindness of the woodland. The softness. The willingness a wood seems to offer to nurture and to forgive, to hold us close when so much in our lives seems too hard, too brittle and too uncaring.

CHAPTER 5

Veg & a bit of fruit

'It's difficult to think anything but pleasant thoughts while eating a homegrown tomato.'

LEWIS GRIZZARD (1946–94)

Most of us are trying to eat more healthily. Whatever that means to you. To me, it's a case of lots more vegetable-based meals, substantially less meat, some fish and complete denial about the vast quantities of cheese I consume on a regular basis.

Growing and eating a rainbow

The idea of following a Mediterranean diet appeals to me on so many levels. We know it's good for us, it's delicious, usually simple to cook or concoct and even if we garden in a tiny patch of land or in pots and tubs, we can grow many of the ingredients we need to eat well. A basil plant on a windowsill, a 'Tumbling Tom' tomato in a hanging basket or – if we are lucky enough to have the space in the garden – a bed full of garlic, courgettes and red onions.

I like the Mediterranean diet not least because I adore olive oil – I'd happily drink it by the pint with a balsamic chaser. My fondness for olive oil is perhaps surprising as, like many Brits of my generation, my early encounters with olive oil were purely medicinal, limited to having it poured, warm, into my Eustachian tube as a cure for earache.

I like the Mediterranean diet not least because I adore olive oil – I'd happily drink it by the pint with a balsamic chaser.

Once administered, the tiny little bottle was rapidly returned to the bathroom cabinet to languish, ignored, behind the claggy Germolene tin and an empty, rancid TCP bottle.

Not only were olives a mystery to most of the population of 1960s' Britain but garlic, too, was a completely alien concept, as were chillies and almost all herbs. Until the age of 15 and a package holiday to Mallorca, a sprig of rosemary on a lamb chop was as close as I got to the Mediterranean, either at the kitchen table or in person. Ah, Mallorca, I will forever be in your debt! Garlic, gazpacho, pimento, the scent of the sea and pine trees carried on the warm evening breeze, a devastatingly handsome Mallorquin fellow, with eyes like burnished bronze and . . . Well. Enough of the delights of my teenage romance. Suffice it to say that it wasn't just the culinary possibilities of adulthood that were revealed to me that summer, but, unlike the fleeting intoxication of a holiday romance, my affection for the intense, heady flavours of Mediterranean cuisine have proved to be a lifelong love affair.

Inspiration closer to home

It's not quite fair to suggest that food back home in Blighty was always awful. Good food was available – a tad bland, perhaps, but the war-time habit of growing vegetables was still ever-present. Digging for Victory was no longer a poster campaign, but self-sufficiency was still very much in the collective consciousness. My family, however, were not gardeners. In fact, my mother used to accuse my father of killing plants just by proximity. 'Freddy! Don't touch anything!' she'd scream out of the bedroom window, as he sloped off, down the narrow strip of grass, past the remaining hydrangea, for a quiet smoke behind the remains of an Anderson shelter. God knows what the neighbours thought he was up to or what it was that he wasn't allowed to touch, but then ours was an unusual household in lots of ways and I suppose they assumed it was just another example of our odd, bohemian lifestyle.

Whenever I think of that slim, barren garden of my childhood, I aways think of Polly Garter in *Under Milk Wood* – 'Nothing grows in our garden, only washing. And babies.' The babies, as I'll explain, were next door at the O'Connors, and long before every home had a tumble drier, line drying meant that all gardens had a good crop of drying clothes. Our garden had a washing line, a wooden bench, two old apple trees and a couple of straggly shrubs. From a horticultural perspective, not much to enjoy, but there was one true delight, the crowning glory of our little suburban garden: a Victoria plum tree. It was tiny and probably quite old, but every July it was festooned with deep purple plums, so many that the overladen branches would bend *almost* low enough for a five-year-old to reach the fruit. Almost low enough but not quite.

While the tree was covered in plums, the honeyed scent and the sweetness of the fruit meant that it was also always fizzing with furious, sugar-crazed wasps. I had to risk climbing up onto a knackered, very wobbly rattan garden chair to get to the ripe treasure. Unsteady but unbowed, once up on the seat, I'd very slowly reach into the cool crumpled leaves with my eager, searching little fingers, gently feeling my way past the furious yellow-and-black stingers to squeeze at a tender plum, which would quietly let go of its hold on the stalk and settle its weight satisfyingly into my plump palm. I honestly don't remember ever being stung. Perhaps the insects were too drunk on plum juice to bother with me or maybe there really was such bounty that they knew there was enough to share. To bite into the softest, sweetest fruit with the unjaded palette of a five-year-old, the warm sun on my back, the sound of chirruping sparrows and the distant whirr of push-along mowers ... not exactly Sissinghurst but a sensory experience that has stayed with me forever.

The beauty and purpose of an allotment

Our next-door neighbours, Mr and Mrs O'Connor, were dedicated serial fosterers. They had grown-up children of their own but there were always umpteen visiting foster children filling every available inch of their house – newborn babies, scrawny under-10s and older children, often including grown-ups – all people who had benefitted from the boundless generosity and love that seemed to envelop the house next door. Kids, teenagers and babies poured out of every door, window, gate and coalhole of number 72. Mr O'Connor was a postal worker and had an allotment. Looking back, I can see that an allotment would have helped feed so many mouths, but perhaps it also served the purpose of preserving an iota of peace and sanity to

Mr O'Connor's life. He must have been grateful on occasion
to get away to the solitude of double-digging and
watering, even for a few hours a week. Allotments
are quite groovy these days and are a regular topic of
discussion at Dalston and Hackney dinner parties.
Hipsters, just like the rest of us, are longing for
the chance to feed their young families, connect
with the earth, the weather and their neighbours
in the truly life-enhancing activity that is growing
your own veg. It's easy to forget that there is nothing
new in the use of allotted land to feed the city
dweller and that, historically, allotments have
been an important part of urban living.

Allotments have existed for hundreds of
years. In the UK there is evidence of allotment-style growing
dating back to Anglo-Saxon times. The way we use allotments now
seems to have its roots, if you'll pardon the pun, in more recent
times, when land was given over to the poor for growing their
own food. This makes perfect sense to me as there was no welfare
state and I imagine no food banks. In 1908, the Small Holdings and
Allotments Act was introduced, meaning that local authorities had a
duty to provide allotments for anyone who needed them. At the end
of the First World War, land was also made available to returning
servicemen. Right up until the present day, the rights of allotment
holders are constantly being strengthened and upheld by law. Indeed,
as of 2018, the Scottish government has required local authorities to
develop a food-growing strategy for their area, including identifying
land that may be used as allotment sites.

Little has changed for hundreds of years in the way that
the allotment system works. Although, back in 1846, parish
law suggested that allotmenteers (if that is a word) were
expected to attend church on a Sunday and anyone who

wanted to 'dig potatoes on a Sunday', had to forfeit their produce as punishment for gardening on the Lord's Day. Interestingly Sundays are now the most popular gardening day of the week.

Fast forward to the present day and you'll see me and lots of others like me enjoying the delights of sowing, planting, harvesting and eating my own fruit and vegetable garden seven days a week, whenever possible. I'm fortunate enough to have a piece of land deep in the heart of rural Devonshire, where I have plenty of room to indulge in my passion for growing. A long and lucky career in television and theatre has allowed me the privilege of having this lovely garden. There are lots of ways to enjoy the fruits of a career like mine – fast cars or diamonds, perhaps? I've gone for a garden instead. I'm not interested in fast cars. Formula 1 doesn't do it for me (F1 hybrids though? Now you're talking!). Diamonds – they might be considered a girl's best friend but on a clear day when the sun sparkles off the windows of the greenhouse? It's all the bling I need.

Back in the 1960s when I was five, the only allotment I'd ever heard of belonged to Mr O'Connor. From time to time, he would bring my family a few of his home-grown vegetables; nothing too exotic, this was post-war Britain after all, but it was all fresh and so tasty: potatoes, sprouts, cabbages and strawberries. I think those strawberries are the reason I garden today.

A list of my favourites

I'm not even going to try and give a comprehensive list of all the diverse, exciting, tasty vegetables and fruits we can grow in our home plots but I thought I'd briefly mention a few of my personal favourites (and one or two that don't really do it for me). There are things I always sow from seed because I can't get through the year without them, some I grow fairly regularly and a few unusual or tricky ones I only attempt when I know I will have a bit more time on my hands, not just to plant but also to harvest, cook and store what I've grown.

Asparagus

I first cooked my favourite asparagus recipe over 20 years ago. Sam and I and our two children, who were very small at the time, were living in a rented cottage in the depths of the Devonshire countryside. The delightful garden had an overgrown patch by some trees and one day, while enjoying the sunshine in early May, I noticed that among the wildflowers and weeds were masses of tall, strong clumps of asparagus spears. It was like finding a treasure chest where you thought there was only an empty cardboard box.

I knew that to cut asparagus properly you find the bottom of the stalk and then cut with a sharp knife just below the surface of the soil. I gathered enough for the four of us and trotted inside to rinse the fresh spears. I can still remember gently steaming that first unexpected crop, drizzling them with a little butter and handing them to the children. They were delicious and the asparagus wasn't bad either.

Little did I know that the surprise asparagus bed was enormous. It had obviously been planted by a keen gardener who knew that the harvesting window for asparagus is short-lived (starting in late April and finishing in mid-June), so it's best to have plenty of crowns. One has to allow some of the asparagus spears to remain unpicked to go to seed, fade to yellow and fall over, so that all of the energy from the

ferns goes back into the asparagus crown to ensure that there will be a
plentiful crop the following year. As I say, this was a large bed and for
six weeks my little family gorged on asparagus in as many ways as it is
possible for asparagus to be eaten: baked in the oven at 180°C (350°F/
Gas Mark 4) for 10 minutes, drizzled with a little olive oil and flaked
salt; or steamed and allowed to cool, served with hollandaise sauce or a
little mayonnaise. We had it in omelettes, in salads and in soups. But
even after all these years, this remains our favourite recipe.

A word to the wise if you haven't eaten asparagus before – it makes
your wee smell. According to some sources this only happens with
certain people. I discovered during that summer all those years ago
that I'm a person who knows they've eaten asparagus. Strong-smelling
wee is a small price to pay, I think, for enjoying a delicious vegetable.
After all, it's only around for a few weeks of the year.

The uncovering of that asparagus bed and the delights of eating a
vegetable that has such a short season and is so simple to cook and enjoy
within minutes of cutting, encouraged me to put an asparagus bed into
my current veg garden. I'm always keen to admit my gardening failures
and so I'll tell you about what a disaster this has been in the hope that
you won't make the same obvious mistake. I built a wooden raised
bed, about 6 x 2 ft (2 x 0.5 m), and filled it with soil. I then purchased
eight really quite expensive asparagus crowns. If you've ever seen an
asparagus crown, you'll understand why I felt totally ripped off when
they arrived in the post. I opened the container to find some spindly,
dry, spidery roots, looking like mummified fingers under wood shavings.
I planted them and waited until the following spring for the first green
tips to poke through the surface of the soil. The veg shops were full of
long, fat, juicy-looking spears but I resisted the temptation to buy, my
heart full of hope. After all, soon I'd have my homegrown asparagus to
feast on, wouldn't I?

Every evening as supper time approached, I'd take a basket and a
curved asparagus knife to the garden, in the hope of gathering my

first crop. I knew that we should leave asparagus to mature and not take too many spears the first year but even if I'd wanted to throw caution to the wind and indulge in a misguided frenzy of harvesting, I wouldn't have been able to. Days passed. April turned in to June and then, finally, just as the very end of the asparagus season approached, three tiny asparagus tips were visible. I waited for a few days and when I could stand the anticipation no longer, I cut the three spears and took them into the kitchen. They were thinner than pencils and as flaccid as shoelaces. I steamed them and ate them alone; this was not the celebratory feast I'd anticipated.

The following year, I waited for the crowns to produce something more robust but again, after a daily vigil during April and June, only a few pathetic spears showed up. At this point I was full of righteous indignation. I blamed the poor-quality crowns, the weather, anything but myself. Then, two years too late, I took advice from a gardening chum. Clearly, I hadn't really done my homework. There was nothing wrong with the crowns I'd bought – they always look DOA, apparently. The problem was all my own making: asparagus needs really good drainage. Who knew? Really good drainage. Not heavy clay soil like mine. Of course, with hindsight, it's obvious. All of the best asparagus is grown in places with sandy, free-draining soil. I should have given it more thought, but I'd rushed ahead, without the right information. In my own defence, I was young (58) and naïve (stupid and arrogant).

Three years ago, I decided to admit defeat and started again with a new bed. I added plenty of grit to the original soil mix and planted (just beneath the surface and not too deeply this time) eight even more eye-wateringly expensive crowns. So far, I've enjoyed a couple of good meals from the new bed and look forward to many more. I keep it well weeded, watered and fed. I hope one day to replicate the abundance of the amazing asparagus bed that I discovered by accident among the weeds, all those years ago. May this woeful tale of my idiocy help you avoid a waste of time and money and enthusiasm and encourage you to start your own asparagus bed. If things go well they should produce abundantly for up to 20 years. I only wish I'd started earlier and not made so many mistakes!

Just before I move on to my next choice of veg, I must tell you, in case you have not thought of it already, that an asparagus spear dipped into the yolk of a runny egg is heaven. Try it instead of the usual buttered toast soldiers. It's far less calorific and if you happen to be a coeliac, as I am, it's an easy swap for bread. There, I've finished talking about asparagus, phew! Sometimes it's not until you tell someone about the object of desire that you realise you are in love. It's good to have got that off my chest.

Garlic

I only grow garlic because I use so much of it in my home cooking. I don't find it particularly easy to grow but I do value it so highly that even after a very poor year I still plant again every November. On my heavy clay soil, I'm never going to achieve great things but if you have a lighter soil and a better-drained site than I, you'll do well if you can get the sunlight to it. I plant in the autumn as garlic likes a spell of cold to form a good bulb with big, fat juicy cloves.

Don't bother sowing from shop-bought cloves as they may carry diseases and produce a poor harvest. I get mine from a well-known grower. They aren't cheap but they are always good quality and even in a wet year I manage a fairly reliable harvest.

Hardneck garlic varieties generally have a stronger flavour and bigger cloves but don't keep as well as the softneck varieties. I think it's worth growing both – I use the hardneck first and plait my softneck heads, using them when I run out of the hardneck bulbs. I tend to cut the hardneck varieties and bunch them like a garlic posey.

I also grow softneck garlic because it stores for longer and I'm a sucker for a plait of homegrown garlic hanging in the kitchen next to homegrown dried chillies.

Here are some hardneck garlic varieties I've had success with: 'Lautrec Wight', 'Chesnok Red' and 'Carcassonne Wight'. My favourite softneck garlic varieties are 'Solent Wight', 'Picardy Wight' and 'Christo'.

Horseradish

When I was young I spoke as a child, I thought as a child, I gardened like a child and took no notice of the advice of more experienced gardeners. Consequently, I have a veg patch totally overrun with horseradish. 'Plant it in a container,' they said. 'Put a membrane down,' they said ... Did I listen? Did I, garden fork. I love horseradish, I'm glad I grow it, but I truly wish I had taken advice. It's a total nuisance of a plant. I'm convinced the reason it's called horseradish is because it gallops all over the garden, leaping fences and, like a Shetland pony, is impossible to control, stubbornly gets into places it shouldn't be and is then impossible to remove. Please do grow it but please, please, save yourself the misery of being overrun and put it in an old dustbin or a big pot. Then you can make the most delicious sauce without waking in a cold sweat from a nightmare because that tapping on the window isn't a ghostly withered hand, it's a big, fat horseradish root, which, triffid-like, has come to claim you for its own and drag you down into its earthy lair.

Purple sprouting broccoli

I've decided to tell you about purple sprouting broccoli instead of green broccoli because it's what I grow. It's packed with vitamins A, B and C, carotenoids, iron, folic acid, calcium and fibre. It also contains phytochemical sulforaphane, which research is revealing may be a useful tool in providing resistance against heart disease and osteoporosis, among other health issues. The first time I ever produced a small crop of this vegetable I felt like a real gardener.

It was a sort of horticultural coming of age. I've always associated brassicas with old men in baggy trousers, braces and flat caps, who whistle tunelessly as they double-dig their allotment. I don't own a flat cap and very rarely wear braces but would happily have donned either garment the day I picked my first bright purple buds of this glorious crop.

If you're lucky enough to have the space to grow this brilliant vegetable, it's worth doing because it can be expensive to buy and it provides delicious pickings when there isn't much else around.

Depending on the variety you can harvest crops from autumn through to early summer the following year. This is a hardy little veg. Sow the seeds in small pots using good-quality seed and cutting compost. Once your seedlings are 10–15 cm (4–6 in) high, harden them off and plant them a little deeper than they've been in the pot. It likes fertile, well-drained soil and will tolerate a little shade. If you're in a windy spot, as I am up here on the hill, try to find a little shelter because, like my cat, Bob, it doesn't like strong winds pushing it around. Any compost will be gratefully received by this plant and if you're generous with the good stuff several months before planting, purple sprouting broccoli will be generous in return.

I always plant leaving plenty of room to reduce the probability of disease and provide an abundance of space for side shoots, giving me larger harvests. Water during a dry spell, pick regularly to prevent bolting and throw a bit of fleece over them if temperatures threaten to get too low.

When the leaves start to turn and the reds and yellows alert me to the fact that autumn is on the way, I stake a few of my broccoli plants just in case gales are imminent.

As to harvesting, it's the simplest and most delicious crop. Sever the small heads (as the proletariat said of the aristocracy in France during the Revolution) and then pop them into a basket.

Steam it, sauté it, stir fry it until tender. It's great as a side dish but also holds its own as a main course. Fresh is best but it will freeze well.

Potatoes

You don't need a massive amount of space to grow potatoes. A large pot will do as long as you can make some drainage holes in the bottom so that watering can be monitored. Too deep a container leaves the top of the soil dry and the bottom wet so the yield will be poor and the quality of your tatties will suffer. Basically, you are aiming for even moistness throughout so that when it comes to harvest you don't find lots of tiny rotting potatoes at the bottom of your pot. Nobody likes a slimy 'Wilja'.

If you are growing directly into the ground, start by deciding what sorts of potatoes you want to grow. There are so many varieties, there's no point devoting your time and energy to something you're not going to use. I grow an early crop (first earlies) because they are harvested in June. Second earlies will be ready soon after and main crop potatoes, which tend to be planted between March and May, are ready to be harvested towards the end of August. Seed potatoes, which are small potato tubers rather than actual seeds, are readily available and a much better option than planting wrinkly old leftover tatties that have produced shoots. These will give you a poor crop.

Chitting

Some people chit their potatoes, some people don't. I'm a chitter – this is not cockney rhyming slang. Chitting involves starting the potatoes in an egg carton, eyes uppermost, then popping them in a cool light place until they start to produce shoots. This can take up to six weeks.

Dig over your soil, remove the weeds and dig trenches 12 cm (5 in) deep and 60 cm (2 ft) apart. Because I'm not good at measuring I tend to do it by eye, so about half a spade deep and two spade lengths apart. The metal blade part obviously, not the whole spade. Plant your seed potatoes about 30 cm (1 ft) apart and refill the trench with soil.

When shoots appear and are about 20 cm (8 in) tall, mound the soil up around the base of the shoots to about halfway up the stems. This is called 'earthing up' and is basically keeping the tiny potatoes in the dark until they are big enough to eat.

   Be careful when you are digging up your potatoes as it's easy to spear your crop with a fork or slice through them with a spade.

Potato varieties

I grow these varieties because I love the flavour and the culinary diversity they provide. There are so many wonderful varieties out there if you have the time and the space – the options are limitless.

'ROCKET': This is a reliable first early, providing a beautiful golden crop of baby new potatoes early in the season. This is a great candidate for containers and potato bag crops.

'NADINE': I grew this for the first time this year as a second early. It seems to be disease resistant and has produced a good crop. It's been very useful as an all-round culinary potato.

'MARIS PIPER': This is an old favourite and for a very good reason. It's invaluable as a baked potato and is excellent for mashing and roasting. These main crop potatoes can get satisfyingly big so I probably wouldn't grow them in a container. Maris pipers are a bit of a lifesaver in the autumn months when people descend on the kitchen and need to be fed after a long walk or a rugby match. Baked potatoes or mounds of mash really do bulk up a meal deliciously and cheaply.

'PINK FIR APPLES': These are a heritage variety and a really useful little potato. They have a nutty flavour and are great boiled, steamed and in salads. They are a late main crop variety but are worth waiting for.

Courgettes

Growing courgettes is a double-edged sword. I don't mean that courgettes can be used as a lethal weapon, obviously, although if you leave them long enough in the ground they can grow to the size of a zeppelin and, if aimed carefully, can be heavy enough to do some serious damage. Courgettes have a habit of either coming to nothing in a bad year or in a good year providing an embarrassment of riches. When the conditions are right it's virtually impossible to keep up with harvesting, cooking or preserving them. It's not as if it's easy to give them away either. I find that a good courgette year for me tends to be a good courgette year for everyone else too. I'm often tempted to leave boxes full of the blighters on doorsteps during the night, so that they are discovered in the morning like abandoned orphans in a Dickens' novel and are taken in by loving parents who have longed for courgettes but have never been blessed with courgettes of their own.

Over the years, when I have been delighted by – or rather plagued by – excess, I have tried to find many different ways to prepare, cook and preserve my courgettes. It just seems so wrong to take the time and effort to raise something from seed and then not eat it. That said, there is absolutely nothing wrong with digging them out and putting them into the compost. If they have really big stems it might be best to chop them up a bit. Here are a couple of ways of dealing with a glut of courgettes:

1   Throw them over the hedge
2   Chargrilled courgettes (see page 100)

Growing courgettes

Start your seeds off between March and May. Pop a single seed into a pot about 1 cm ($^1/_3$ in) deep and either cover with a lid or a plastic bag. Keep moist and keep your eyes open because pretty soon, if they're in a sunny spot, a green shoot will appear. Once they get going, move them into larger pots and either keep them in the greenhouse or, when frosts have passed, they can go outside. They need plenty of room so give them at least 2 ft (60 cm) between plants. Keep them well watered, remain vigilant for slug attacks and soon you will be eating your first yellow or green torpedoes.

It is possible to grow courgettes successfully in containers. The variety 'Midnight' is famously compact and therefore a good one if you're limited for space. The ball-shaped courgette 'Eclipse' is fun and a little different too.

Globe artichokes

Until a couple of years ago I had never grown a globe artichoke. I had grown a relative, the cardoon, as an ornamental plant in the border of a city garden many moons ago. I believe they are also edible, but I guess life was busy back then and I didn't get around to trying them in the kitchen. Cardoons are as beautiful as they are architectural, so if you don't fancy the globe artichoke, these plants really do make an impact in a border. My devotion to the artichoke began with my lovely postie, Paul, who offered me a couple of artichoke plants. Small and unremarkable, I put them into my veg plot. I had no idea at the time that within a few years they would become one of the real high points of my gardening year.

If you have room and a sunny spot with relatively free-draining soil, then I really think they are worth a go, not least because they are just divine to look at. They disappear under the earth during winter and, as the soil warms, they start to come through again and remind you of their stately, rather noble, presence. Once they get going, they gallop away. Their big grey-green and purple heads develop quickly into huge, hard, spiky heads, the plump, thick, fleshy leaves standing high and proud on a strong, ridged stem. If you let them flower, and I really strongly suggest that you do, they are even more beautiful. Their heads burst into colour, revealing their true thistle nature.

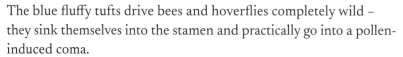

The blue fluffy tufts drive bees and hoverflies completely wild – they sink themselves into the stamen and practically go into a pollen-induced coma.

It's not only the insects that appreciate the flowering artichokes. I think they are one of the most fabulous additions to the garden. For me they are the perfect veg-garden, potager or flower-garden plant. They just keep delivering in a myriad of ways: the leaves, the rigid stems, the whole glorious heavy heads towering over the other vegetables. Then, joy of joys, the flowers: vibrant, papal-purple in the summer-evening light.

When the heads are small, about the size of a lemon, they are remarkably easy to cook in the Italian style.

Jerusalem artichokes

The windy one. Anyone who has ever eaten Jerusalem artichokes, either roasted or as a creamy soup, will testify that they are delicious but that you really must be prepared for the most astounding bouts of wind. They are called fartichokes in my house and for very good reason. Jerusalem artichokes contain high levels of inulin, a non-digestible carbohydrate fermented by gut bacteria.

It's best to weigh the pot down with a couple of bricks or similar. One of my infamous gluten-free Victoria sponges would be ideal.

These are relatives of the sunflower. Plant the tubers in just the way you'd plant potatoes, directly outdoors in late winter or early spring. You will be harvesting in the late autumn. Just dig them up and use them as you need them. I always leave a few tubers in the ground and they provide a crop the following year. This is great if you have room but a pain in the neck if you don't, as they will turn up mob-handed if you don't get most of the tubers up at the end of the season. The stems can get very tall and might need a bit of help to keep them upright. A well-placed stake will do the trick. They do well in my clay soil in Devon, but I don't believe they are too fussy as long as they aren't waterlogged – but then none of us really enjoy that, do we? That said, if it's really dry, do water them as they need it to swell the tubers. Some people take the yellow flowers off to send the energy down to the tuber. I leave most of mine as I can't resist the beauty of their little gold faces and because they continue to flower well into autumn and the late bees love them.

WARNING – if you do have a small garden I'd advise growing these in a large container – they can really be pretty thuggish given the right conditions. One good-sized tuber per pot and a mix of garden soil and peat-free compost. Beware of wind . . . No, not that kind – I've already mentioned that – the other kind. A high wind will knock the container over as they do get tall. It's best to weigh the pot down with a couple of bricks or similar. One of my infamous gluten-free Victoria sponges would be ideal.

Beetroot

My husband, Sam, HATES beetroot. I don't care. I grow it because it is, in my opinion one the finest things that has ever happened to me. Sam is also one of the finest things that has ever happened to me but please don't ask me to choose between the two.

I've never tried to cover him in olive oil and feta and roast him but I think we all know who'd win that contest.

Carrots

A packet of 250 carrot seeds will set you back a couple of quid. In return you can expect about 200 carrots and hours of pleasure spent in the spring sunshine, succession planting. Enjoy them raw, roasted and boiled, as crudité with dips and also in warming winter stews. If you grow them in heavier soils or in stony ground you might get the funny misshapen two- or three-legged roots. I quite like a few 'running men' in my harvest but if you prefer something easier to prep then good soil and drainage is important.

Peas

I'm almost too angry to write this, as I've just been outside to discover that *none* of my recently planted peas have survived. Will I never learn?

Mice eat 80 per cent of the peas I sow directly outside. I still try growing them like this because hope springs eternal in the human breast but I also back up my planting by sowing plenty in the greenhouse too. Mice eat 40 per cent of the peas I plant in the greenhouse.

I have five cats, five . . . where the hell are all these mice coming from?

Mice + peas = happy mice and no peas for the wicked.

Sowing peas directly outside (to feed mice and shrews)

I grow peas in three rows, stagger the seeds so they are about 7.5 cm (3 in) apart, cover them with soil, lightly firm them in, water well and wait for them to be eaten by rodents.

There are many different varieties of peas and various sizes – some get as tall as 1.8 m (6 ft) and then there are the dwarf varieties that come in at about 45 cm (18 in). As well as the different heights, just like potatoes, there are early varieties and main crop varieties, mange tout and sugar snaps. All peas like a sunny position and good drainage and prefer a neutral or slightly alkaline soil. They don't like competition so weed well before you plant them. Pop in something for them to climb up (pea sticks as opposed to pooh sticks). If you really do struggle to grow peas in the garden because of rodents you can put a single pea into a single module and cover with sowing compost. Water and wait with bated breath and baited traps.

Or start indoors: get a piece of plastic guttering. Drill drainage holes (it's a pain to do but this guttering will last for years). Fill it with soil, zig-zag the peas (as you'd do outside) and water. When the shoots start to appear and look strong and tough enough not to appeal to little teeth, push the 'plug' of plant out as one long piece into a pre-prepared trench outside.

Jalapeño peppers

I grow jalapeños every year, along with lots of different sorts of chillies. Unfortunately, I have found that there is no way of knowing, until you put it in your mouth, the intensity of the heat in each little pepper. That said, if you like a little zing on your tongue, jalapeños are the plant for you. The same plant will produce a variety of different levels of heat. Try my brilliant little dish of Jalapeño pepper poppers (see page 98) for an element of Russian roulette.

Leeks

There is something so satisfying about digging up a home-grown leek. I started growing them just a couple of years ago. With their mild onion flavour and upright habit, I love to see their blue-green leaves standing to attention, ready to be harvested in the autumn. Or you can leave them standing through the colder months and lift when you need them. I sow mine indoors, usually early in the year from February to March, and then transplant them once I've hardened them off, gradually acclimatising them by keeping them in a cold frame that I open during the day. Until this year I have always 'puddled in' my leeks – standing a single leek in a hole I make with a dibber and then filling the hole with water, allowing the soil to gently settle around the roots. This year, however, I watched a YouTube video in which a man who grows leeks professionally (he grows thousands of them every year) pops three or four leeks together into a hole before 'puddling in'. It seems to make little difference when it comes to the quality of the produce but it really speeds up the planting. I just gently extricated the plug of leeks from the cell tray (each containing three or four leeks) and, rather than separating them into individuals, I popped the whole plug into the hole. As I write we are in midsummer – I'm keeping the plot fairly weed-free and I'm going to see if this more time-effective method works.

If you want a longer white shank on your leeks, once they are looking pretty sturdy, start earthing up a little around them. Remember they do love a drink so don't let them dry out.

During the winter months it's so handy to have leeks in the garden. As with most veg, I prefer not to mess about with them too much, particularly if they've come from the garden. Chop off the dark-green leaves – these are too tough to eat – then trim off the root end (but hang on to all this because it's brilliant for adding to a vegetable stock – see page 109 for my homemade veg stock recipe). Cut the leeks in half lengthways and wash very carefully, making sure to get rid of all the grit and soil trapped between the beautiful, translucent, pale layers. Once they're prepped, slice them and pop them into a heavy-bottomed pan with a knob of butter and a little oil to stop the butter from burning. Put them on a low heat, put a lid on the pan and check regularly to make sure they're not catching. Add a little salt and pepper if you like and they are the most brilliant side dish.

Broad beans

I'm not a fan of these. Sam, my husband, likes them, so here goes. I used to grow them and then spend the best part of spring trying to keep the tiny black beetles off them, staking them, blanching the tiny first beans and slipping them out of their leathery, bitter little jackets, only to be left with such tiny little fingernail-sized green split beans that I resented every mouthful of the salad or risotto I'd used them in. There I've said it. Cancel me, excommunicate me, divorce me, do what you will. I can't be bothered with them anymore. I'm too old and have too much else to achieve in what's left of my life.

Runner beans

Runner beans are so beautiful that even if we didn't eat them, I'd still have some in the garden. I often grow a red-and-white variety up a wigwam or tunnel of canes. The flowers are so perfect and the leaves sit so elegantly on the sinuous stem that reaches for the sky, producing bunches of long, green, entirely edible pods. I try to pick mine before they get too big and tough, particularly if it's a good harvest, as they are great to slice and blanche (put briefly into boiling water and then briefly into iced water) and then freeze in portion-sized bags. I don't do much with them, fresh or frozen – I just add butter, salt and pepper.

Runner beans are so beautiful that even if we didn't eat them, I'd still have some in the garden.

Rhubarb

Like asparagus, rhubarbs are grown from a crown. Over the years I've had some successes and failures with rhubarb – sad to report, mostly failures.

Rhubarb, to flourish, needs an open sunny site, with moist but free-draining soil. It doesn't like being waterlogged – again, who does? It also hates a late frost, which will damage young growth.

Plant dormant crowns in November in a hole deep enough to take the whole crown, leaving just the tips visible. If you have access to some well-rotted manure, it gives the plant a really good start. If not, then use good-quality compost. Because I live on a heavy clay soil, the advice is to leave a little more of the plant peeping above the surface of the earth to avoid the whole thing rotting away. That said, avoid letting your rhubarb dry out. Once it starts to grow, if you hit a dry spell, water regularly.

Despite having followed this good advice, the three new crowns I planted this year still look a little puny. I shall persevere, give them a good feed in the spring and hopefully get more big, strong, pink-and-green stems as the years go by. Every year my rhubarb crowns, both new and old, throw up big, bobbly flower stalks. I now remove these as they reduce the vigour of the plant. I may only get a few decent-sized stalks every year but I will keep going because they are so delicious.

When harvesting it's important to leave new crowns virtually untouched. I allow myself to take one or two stems but it really is best to limit yourself for the first few years. Likewise, forcing young rhubarb plants isn't a good idea. This is the practice of 'forcing' the plant to search for light by keeping it in the dark, under a bucket or a terracotta pot. Rhubarb stems should be pulled rather than cut. Take your hand down the silky rhubarb stem until you reach the base, very close to the crown. Grip tightly and, with a quick, firm action, pull the stem up and away. I am aware this may sound like something from the 1970s' *Joy of Sex* manual but I'm afraid there is no getting away from the fact this is the best way to avoid the crown rotting away in damp weather.

Raspberries

Raspberries are relatively easy to grow. If, like me, you get tired of the mouldy mushy mess that you bring home from the shops, it's great to have access to a fresh reliable supply of berries. Raspberries are split into 'summer-fruiting' and 'autumn-fruiting' types. Summer-fruiting raspberries fruit on the previous year's growth and are typically tall plants that require staking. Autumn-fruiting raspberries are shorter and usually less vigorous, and fruit on the current season's growth. Growing a combination of the two types means you can harvest your own raspberries from late June through to October. Grow raspberries in moist but well-drained, fertile soil in full sun to partial shade.

Redcurrants

The glorious, shiny, translucent clusters of berries on a redcurrant bush are one of the most striking things ever to adorn a garden. Even if they weren't a fabulous culinary plant I'd still grow them because of the extravagant beauty they bring. Their ruby red berries remind me of the jewels that adorn Henry VIII's costume in the famous Holbein portrait of 1540. Redcurrants have an inner glow that makes them look as if they are lit from within.

As with other berries, if you resent sharing them with the birds, it's best to net them. They are easy to plant and, once they are in, they require virtually no looking after and will reward you or the blackbirds with up to 4.5 kg (10 lbs) of currants each summer. If you've room for red, then why not grow whitecurrants and blackcurrants, too? They are all easy and useful.

Strawberries

I have a strawberry bed in my garden in Devon just as I have an asparagus bed and a rhubarb patch – these are permanent fixtures. Asparagus plants will last for years, as will rhubarb crowns. Strawberries on the other hand will produce fruit for around four years, which isn't very long, but they do reward us with free plants by throwing out runners – horizontal stems that run above the ground and produce new plants.

If you have room, it's worth giving strawberries a go. They take up little space so are great in containers and even hanging baskets, and if you plant several varieties, you can have home-grown harvests from early summer through to autumn. Plant in a sheltered, sunny or lightly shaded spot. Water and weed regularly and protect the fruits from birds, slugs and snails and you'll be enjoying plump, red, juicy fruits as the first tennis ball bounces off the first racket in the Wimbledon fortnight.

From the hedgerow

Blackthorns
In the early spring, some of the first blossom to appear is the frothy white lace of the blackthorn. Later in the year it will become small deep purple-blue berries, each covered in a soft bloom. To my mind there is nothing that marks the change of season from autumn to winter like the yearly excursion to pick the sloe berries that grow on the blackthorn bush. Beware, the blackthorn gets its name from the long, incredibly sharp thorns that protect the berries on the bough. Heading out to pick sloes in the early winter time is one of the constant rhythms of country life.

Elderflower
Before the blue-black berries of the elder hang heavy in the hedgerows, the creamy-yellow elderflowers are an early sign of summer. They are a brilliant source of food for insects and make a delicious, thirst-quenching cordial for humans. Make sure, if you're going to harvest some elderflower heads, that you take them from quite high up the plant as you don't want any that have been near car fumes or dog wee. As with any hedgerow bounty, take the freshest and best and no more than you need.

CHAPTER 6

My favourite recipes

'I like the Mediterranean diet not least because I adore olive oil – I'd happily drink it by the pint with a balsamic chaser.'

CAROLINE QUENTIN

Jalapeño pepper poppers

Serves 2; *ideally with a cold beer on a hot day*

8 jalapeño chilli peppers – *I allow 4 chillies per person, so 8 halves. I know it sounds like a lot but it's never enough.*
2 unsmoked back bacon rashers

A handful of grated mature Cheddar cheese
165 g (5¾ oz/scant ¾ cup) cream cheese

1   Preheat the oven to 180°C (350°F/Gas Mark 4).

2   Rinse the chillies under a cold tap, then slice them lengthways, trying to slice through the stalk too, so that you have a little handle to lift the chilli into your mouth. Deseed the halved peppers carefully using the handle of a teaspoon, taking care not to damage the integrity of the skin and taking even greater care not to touch your face.

3   Fry the bacon to your liking – in this recipe, I don't like it crispy. Leave the rashers to cool, then cut into tiny pieces – the smaller the pieces, the easier it is to stuff the peppers.

4   Stir the Cheddar into the cream cheese, then mix in the bacon bits. (If you make these once, you'll make them again. Play around with the amounts of cheese and bacon to suit your taste.)

5   Fill the little green cases with the mixture (I use 2 teaspoons per half pepper and make a right mess), then arrange on a baking tray. Place in the preheated oven for 15–20 minutes or until golden brown.

6   Serve the jalapeños to your guests; I'd advise having a glass of milk (and a swear box) handy just in case.

Chargrilled courgettes   Serves 2

1 kg (2¼ lb) courgettes (zucchini)   **To serve (optional)**
Olive oil, for brushing   Sherry vinegar
Chopped fresh herbs   Balsamic vinegar
                                           Crushed garlic
                                           Salt and pepper

I use some of the more overgrown, bigger courgettes for this recipe. It's so easy, it's not really a recipe at all but it's a delicious way of using up courgettes and feeding lots of people cheaply and easily, particularly during barbecue season. This dish is delicious hot or cold. I prefer mine cold as they develop a better texture (I think) as they cool. If you don't want to use them straight away, they will keep in the fridge overnight and are really handy for big summer gatherings. I sometimes serve them with griddled peppers because the colours are spectacular. This will feed two people, but as I say, just double up as you need. It really does bulk up a meal and it's a good way of getting veg into the family.

1   To prepare the courgettes, top and tail them, but don't peel. Cut
     them lengthways into slices about 1 cm (½ in) thick. Brush or rub
     a little olive oil onto both sides of the slices.

2   Preheat a griddle or non-stick frying pan over a high heat. Add
     the courgettes and sear for a few minutes, turning from time to
     time. They'll be ready in about 5–10 minutes, depending on their
     size, when they are softened and char lines appear on the slices.

3   Serve them with any or all of the above suggestions, and
     sprinkled with fresh herbs.

Purple sprouting broccoli with chilli, garlic and lemon

Serves 4

A slug of olive oil
Fresh stems of purple sprouting broccoli
(*I allow about five per person*)
1 fresh chilli, very finely chopped
(*I'll leave it up to you as to how much you
want to use. My husband will quite happily
eat the chilli and not bother with the broccoli
but you know your family and friends best.*)

2 cloves of garlic (*or more if you can't get
enough of it, which I certainly can't*)
Finely grated zest and juice of 1
unwaxed lemon
Salt and pepper

*This is a recipe that I gave to a friend's little boy, a fussy eater, when he was
about four years old. Yes, I even included a tiny bit of very finely chopped chilli.
I often think some children turn their noses up at vegetables because we assume
that they prefer bland foods, whereas often I think the reverse is true. Adults
adore it too.*

1   Heat the olive oil in a large frying pan or a wok over a medium
     heat. Throw in the broccoli and stir fry until it starts to catch and
     turn golden brown – about 5 minutes.

2   Add the chilli, garlic and lemon zest and keep it all moving rapidly
     around the pan for 1 minute – DON'T BURN THE GARLIC!

3   Add half a cup of water, cover with a lid, some foil or a plate, and
     steam until tender – about 3 minutes.

4   Season and serve with the lemon juice poured over, and enjoy
     getting all your vitamins in the best way possible.

Asparagus and pea risotto   Serves 4

2 handfuls of frozen peas (*or fresh if you're lucky enough to have some*)

1 onion

300 g (10½ oz/1½ cups) risotto rice (such as Arborio)

1.5 litres (52 fl oz/6½ cups) hot vegetable stock (*see page 109 for homemade*)

Asparagus (*obviously! I allow 3 large spears per person but it's entirely up to you*)

A large knob (*if that's not too Benny Hill*) of butter (roughly 50 g/1¾ oz/3½ tbsp), plus a little for cooking the sage

175 ml (6 fl oz/¾ cup) white wine (or vermouth)

2 handfuls of grated Parmesan (*to finish the dish*)

A handful of sage, rough stalks removed and leaves finely shredded

Salt and pepper

This recipe converts well to a chicken dish, and leeks, mushrooms, spinach, broad beans and thinly sliced runner beans all work well too. If you don't grow your own asparagus, it really doesn't matter as it's usually readily available in supermarkets and, despite losing the absolute joy of that plot to plate flavour, it is still one of the finest things you'll ever eat.

It's best to prep everything beforehand and have it handy as it will go straight into the pan. I always start by making a big saucepan of vegetable stock. Occasionally when I come over all Martha Stewart, I make my own (see page 109 for this recipe). Otherwise, you can use good-quality stock cubes, pots or bouillon. It's useful to have either a ladle or a little jug handy because you'll be adding the stock little by little as it gets absorbed by the rice.

1   Prepare your ingredients: take your frozen peas out of the freezer and let them defrost. Finely chop the onion. Measure out the risotto rice. Grate the parmesan into a small bowl. Bring your stock to just below boiling and keep it hot.

2   To prepare the asparagus, first take off the woodier, pale ends of the stalks (the bits that were under the earth). Cut off the growing tips – the top 5 cm (2 in) – and keep these separate. They go in last because they are tender and go mushy if cooked for too long. Now wash the lot under a cold tap.

3   Heat the butter in a large frying pan and gently fry the onion over a medium–low heat until soft – be sure not to let it catch and turn brown. Add the asparagus stalks and cook for 4–5 minutes.

4   Add the rice and cook for about a minute. When it looks translucent (after a minute or two), add the wine, then add a small amount of hot stock. Keep cooking and stirring until most of the liquid is absorbed before gradually adding the rest of the stock.

5   After 15 minutes or so, you will have a tired arm and hopefully most of the stock will have been absorbed and the rice will be almost tender – if it's a bit brittle and hard, cook and stir a little longer. Now add the peas and the asparagus tips and cook for a further 5 minutes until the rice is tender.

6   Take the pan off the heat, stir in the Parmesan and add a little salt and pepper, if you think it needs it.

7   Melt a little butter in a small frying pan and fry the sage leaves for 1–2 minutes until just golden – drizzle the sage butter and leaves over the risotto and serve.

Creamed horseradish sauce   Makes about 350g (12⅓ oz)

4 tbsp grated fresh horseradish   ½ tbsp English mustard
2 tbsp crème fraîche   A pinch of sugar
2 tbsp double (heavy) cream   Salt

This is another of those recipes that divides the family. Let's face it – you either like horseradish or you don't. If you do, please try this. It's great with beef, obviously, but I really think it comes into its own with mackerel, either fresh and straight off a barbecue or on smoked fillets straight out of the packet.

Dig up either a medium-sized root or a few smaller roots, wash thoroughly and grate. Please take care as later in the season the roots can produce fumes that really make your eyes water.

1   Mix everything together in a bowl and add salt to taste.

2   Store in a tightly sealed jar in the fridge. I've often kept mine for up to a month. I understand it can keep longer but I love to eat it fresh so tend to make smaller batches on the day for specific meals.

TIP Did you know that horseradish is high in calcium, magnesium, potassium and vitamin C? However, it's not good for people with stomach ulcers or inflammatory bowel disease, and if you have kidney problems, it is best avoided.

Sautéed baby artichokes with lemon and garlic

4 tbsp olive oil (*dont be afraid to add more if you need, you'll only live longer!*)
Juice of ¹/₂ lemon, plus a squeeze for the artichoke water and extra to serve

8 baby artichokes
2 cloves of garlic, finely chopped
Salt and black pepper

1   In a medium-sized bowl, combine the olive oil, lemon juice and a pinch of salt.

2   Trim the artichokes: cut off the top third, remove the spiky bits and trim away the outer leaves, until you see the pale, soft leaves. If it seems as though you are throwing away half the plant, you are! Halve the heads lengthways and put them into a bowl of cold water that has a squeeze of lemon juice in it – this stops them oxidising and turning brown while you work. Next, drain the artichokes and slide them into the oily mixture, tossing to make sure they are thoroughly coated.

3   Heat a non-stick pan over a medium heat. Place the well-oiled little beauties into the hot pan with the garlic and fry gently for 3 minutes, until golden brown. Add a splash of water and continue to cook for 2 minutes. Flip them over and repeat the process. If they are tender enough to pierce with a fork, they are ready to be eaten. A squeeze of fresh lemon and a twist of black pepper is all they need.

Roasted beetroot, onion and garlic   Serves 2

Olive oil, for greasing
4 small beetroots, washed, trimmed
   and quartered
2 small onions, peeled and quartered

8 cloves of garlic (*I don't bother to
   peel mine*)
A handful of fresh or dried thyme,
   or herb of your choice

This is the most ridiculously simple and utterly delicious meal. If you wanted to make it more substantial, crumbling a little feta over the hot roasted vegetables is bloody marvellous.

1   Preheat your oven to 190°C (375°F/Gas Mark 5).

2   Grab a sheet of kitchen foil about 75 cm (30 in) long, or use a roasting dish with a lid. Grease your foil or dish with a little olive oil.

3   Place all of the ingredients in the middle of the foil and scrunch it up, leaving a little room for steam to circulate. (*This always reminds me of the spotted handkerchief that Puss in Boots tied to the end of his stick when he was accompanying Dick Whittington to London.*) Or place the lid on the dish.

4   Place the vegetable parcel on a baking tray in the preheated oven for 35–45 minutes. Test the beetroot by prodding it rudely with a fork – if it's tender, you're good to go. (Be careful when you open the package as the steam will hit you in the face.)

5   Squeeze the garlic cloves out of their skin and spread over crusty bread, or just mix the garlic into the other vegetable juices before dividing between plates to serve.

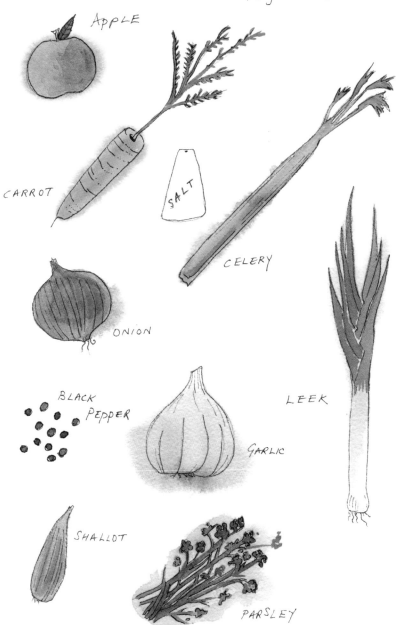

VEGETABLE STOCK

APPLE

CARROT

SALT

CELERY

ONION

BLACK PEPPER

GARLIC

LEEK

SHALLOT

PARSLEY

Vegetable stock

Makes about 1.5 litres (51 fl oz)

3 onions and/or 6 shallots, skin on
3 large carrots
2 celery stalks

A fistful of parsley, thyme or other fresh herbs
6 whole black peppercorns

Rather than buying cubes or little plastic pots, you can make your own delicious basic stock using whatever you have handy. That said, don't put in potatoes or squashes as they make the stock cloudy. I'd also advise against using the leafy parts of carrots and celery or any brassicas, turnips or kale or green beans. What I love about this is that I don't have to use any salt and I can decide what flavours to add when I'm cooking the final dish. Mushrooms are a great addition, too, but because I don't grow them I often don't have any handy.

1   Rinse any soil off the vegetables and roughly chop everything. Throw it all into the biggest pot you've got and cover with enough water to make stirring them easy (about 2 litres/70 fl oz/8¾ cups).

2   Put the pot over a medium–high heat and, once the water starts to bubble, turn it down to a gentle simmer and cook for about an hour. As with all my recipes, this isn't an exact science, so keep an eye on it.

3   Take it off the heat, remove all the vegetables with a slotted spoon and strain over a bowl. Some people use a cheesecloth but I don't mind a few little bits.

4   If I'm not using it immediately, I freeze it, having made sure it's completely cool before I divide it up into small batches and pop it in the freezer.

Rosemary jelly

A large handful of Rosemary Sprigs (*a lovely actress*)

900 g (2 lb) sour cooking apples, chopped

About 900 g (2 lb/4½ cups) granulated sugar (see method below)

Juice of 1 lemon

If you have time, energy and six medium-sized jars, this rosemary jelly is divine. I find a dessert spoon of this in any gravy is one of the best secret weapons in my kitchen. I pride myself on delicious gravies but truthfully, it's all about the jelly.

1   Preheat the oven to 150°C (300°F/Gas Mark 2).

2   Strip the rosemary leaves from the stalks and scatter on a baking sheet. Place in the preheated oven for 30 minutes. Once dried, take them out and put them to one side.

3   Put the chopped apples (cores and pips included) into a preserving pan – something with a heavy bottom (*like Rosemary Sprigs, the really lovely actress*). Pour in 1.5 litres (52 fl oz/6½ cups) of water and the roasted rosemary stalks. Bring the apples to the boil, simmering gently for 30–40 minutes until they have turned to mush.

4   Mash the apples up – I use a potato masher – then put the lot into a muslin cloth or a jelly bag, dangle it over a bowl and leave overnight.

5   Measure the strained juice and calculate the amount of sugar needed – for every 600 ml (21 fl oz/2½ cups) of juice use 450 g (1 lb/2¼ cups) of sugar.

6   Put the strained juice and sugar in a saucepan and add the lemon juice and the dried rosemary leaves. Set over a moderate heat, stirring until all the sugar is dissolved, then bring to a rolling boil and cook for 20 minutes or until the jelly reaches setting point (see Tip below).

7   Let the jelly cool for 10 minutes, then ladle it into warm, sterilised jars. Store in a cool, dark place and refrigerate after opening.

TIP   As with jams and other jellies, to check the jelly is set put three saucers or side plates into the fridge and do the setting test. Drip a little mixture onto the very cold plate, then tip the plate to see if the mixture is runny. If it thickens and wrinkles a little when you push it with your finger, then it is ready to put into the jars. If not, keep cooking and testing frequently.

Rhubarb vodka   Makes 1 litre (34 fl oz)

---

800 g (1³/₄ lbs) chunky pieces of rhubarb   250 g (1 ¹/₄ cups) caster (superfine) sugar
1 litre (35 oz) vodka (*don't spend a fortune,*
  it's not worth it)

---

1   Put the rhubarb in a large bowl and pour in the vodka and sugar.

2   Stir the mixture until the sugar has dissolved, then pour into a
     2-litre (4-pint) sterilised jar with a rubber sealed lid.

3   Leave to infuse in a cool, dark place for at least 8–9 weeks.

4   Strain through a muslin cloth into sterilised, sealable bottles.

Rhubarb martini   Makes 1

---

2 measures rhubarb vodka   Ice
½ measure dry vermouth   Twist of lemon or lime peel

---

1   Put the rhubarb vodka, dry vermouth and a little ice in a cocktail
     shaker. Give it a good Tom Cruise-style shake. Strain into a chilled
     martini glass and serve with a twist of lemon or lime peel.

Redcurrant vodka

Makes about 1.5–2 litres (51–68 fl oz)

750 g (1½ lb/4 cups) redcurrants
750 ml (26 fl oz) vodka

300 g (10½ oz/1½ cups) caster
(superfine) sugar
150 ml (5 fl oz) water

*I have a chickenwire-covered space in my garden that I rather grandly call
a fruit cage. In it are various bushes; redcurrants, blueberries, blackberries
and whitecurrants. Redcurrant jelly is fabulous with lamb and cold cuts but
sometimes I get such a stonking good crop that I am forced into using up some
of the shiny scarlet berries to make redcurrant vodka. It is without doubt one of
the most vibrant, sexy, glamourous things that ever enters my pantry.*

1   Put the redcurrants and vodka into a big glass jar, seal the lid and
     leave somewhere dark for 3 months.

2   After 3 months, empty the mixture into a large bowl, mash it
     together, then filter the mixture through muslin, a sieve or a
     filter bag.

3   In a saucepan, add sugar to the water and dissolve on a low heat to
     make a syrup.

4   Add the syrup to the fruit/vodka mix and pour into a sterilised jar

5   Leave in a cool dark place for at least 2 months (*or 6 minutes if you
     can't stand the wait*).

6   Decant into sterilised bottles.

Sloe gin   Makes about 1.5 litres (51 fl oz)

---

500 g (1 lb/1¾ cups) sloe berries
250 g (9 oz/1¼ cups) caster
  (superfine) sugar

1 litre (35 fl oz) gin (*cheap and cheerful*
  is best)

---

*If you've never made your own sloe gin you're in for a treat. The flavour is
unique – soft, sweet and musty, it murmurs the memories of wood fires, sharp
frosts and clear, cold starry nights.*

1   Rinse the sloes. Pat them dry and prick each berry using a needle
      or a cocktail stick, to infuse the gin. *Alternatively, if you don't have
      the time or the inclination to prick each sloe by hand, put them in the
      freezer overnight. They will split, achieving the same result.*

2   Put the pricked or frozen sloes into an airtight glass jar, add the
      sugar and pour in the gin.

3   Place the jar in a dark, cool place, preferably somewhere where
      you won't forget about it, as for the first 2 weeks it's good to
      agitate the jar every day or so.

4   When the sugar has dissolved, ignore it, I mean really pay it no
      heed. Treat it like it's someone who offended you many years
      ago and whom you have decided to erase from your memory.
      I'm being quite strict about this because *under no circumstances
      should you have anything to do with your gin jar until 12 months at
      least have passed.*

5   When you can bear it no longer
     and you've decided to let bygones
     be bygones and throw your arms
     around your old friend, then –
     and only then – can you strain
     the mixture through some
     muslin and decant it into two
     clean bottles.

CHAPTER 7

Pets & pests

'Where is the poet fired to sing
The snail's discreet degrees,
A rhapsody of sauntering,
A gloria of ease …'

THE SNAIL BY E.V. LUCAS (1868–1938)

Just as with human beings, one man's best friend is another woman's irritating football bore. So I find with both pets and pests. For instance, as many of you know from my Instagram account, I have five cats. To some people, these five cats would be considered pests. To me they are pets and, on many occasions, complete pests. I think it is not by chance that pest is an anagram of pets. I know of people (and there are plenty of them, you'd be surprised) who keep snails as pets: massive African snails, tiny garden snails, water snails, but nonetheless they are snails. Just as there are websites devoted to keeping snails as pets, there are, I imagine many more websites devoted to eliminating snails from our gardens – you take my point.

I think it is not by chance that pest is an anagram of pets.

I am not aware of anyone who keeps slugs as pets but then until recently, when I was searching for a short garden hoe, I was unaware of what some people get up to in the privacy of their own back yards. It's made me look at rubberised gardening gloves in a whole new way.

Raining cats and dogs

Lots of us gardeners try to combine being good pet owners with being good gardeners. As well as five cats, I also have two dogs, both bitches, and, as anyone with a lawn will tell you, the yellow patch a female dog can make on a lawn, usually days before visitors arrive, is an unsightly thing. I now know this is not entirely true as the urine of male dogs does exactly the same thing, only because they don't squat but lift their legs the impact isn't so great. There are several ways of dealing with this problem. It turns out some sorts of grass are more sensitive to dog wee than others but if, like me, you're not sure what the lawn is made up of, this doesn't really help. So it seems that if you have a real problem with this, there is now a task-specific bacterial spray.

Patch-be-gone

1   Spray the offending brown patch with copious amounts of water
     ASAP to neutralise the urine.
2   Spreading horticultural lime or adding powdered gypsum to the
     water will neutralise the acid.

I've also heard of ways to treat the problem from the inside out, as
it were. These are supplements you can feed your dog. I wouldn't
personally use these as I love my dogs much more than I love my lawn
and, to be honest, No Mow May means that I now treat what used to
be a lawn more like a meadow and the bees, the butterflies, the dogs
and the humans are all much happier.

   Cats can seek out a newly dug piece of earth like an Influencer
can sniff out a PR opportunity. This has created problems for
me as I expand my vegetable-growing hobby. A word of warning.
Many years ago, I discovered during a routine blood test in my first
pregnancy that I had toxoplasmosis antibodies in my bloodstream,
which meant that at some point I'd had toxoplasmosis. Had I still
been infected with toxoplasmosis when I fell pregnant, I would
have had a serious problem. The chance of getting toxoplasmosis
for the first time during pregnancy is thought to be very small and
touching contaminated cat poo (for example, by changing the litter
box and then touching your mouth or touching food) is unlikely
to happen. Likewise eating vegetables that have contaminated soil
on them. Nonetheless it would be remiss of me not to mention
this to anyone who gardens, particularly anyone who has cats and
might be pregnant or planning to become pregnant. If you have any
doubts about this at all I suggest going to either the NHS website or
Tommy's: Together for Every Baby.

   So, even without the risk of toxoplasmosis, none of us want to
eat vegetables that have been anywhere near animal faeces. It's hard
enough when it's your own animals but really frustrating if it's visiting

moggies and you're a cat hater or a bird lover. I have a few suggestions before I tell you how I deal with it.

Cat-off

1   Some people use something called a 'sacrificial bed' – a piece of dug earth that you make available for one purpose and one purpose only.

2   Keep beds watered well; they don't like damp soil.

3   Keep a water squirter or hose handy and, though you won't catch them every time in the act as it were, catch them often enough with a short sharp jet of cold water up the tail end and they will soon associate you with an enema they didn't ask for.

4   Chicken-wire fences that lean towards the direction the cat approaches from will be virtually impossible to scale.

5   In this part of the world Devon gamekeepers use light reflection as a deterrent by half-filling bottles of water that catch the light. I imagine mirrors might do the same thing but I have a cat, Ottoline, that is so vain she would spend days watching herself urinate and think it utterly beguiling.

6   There are ultrasonic cat deterrents, which, if you go to the RSPB website, will give you more information.

7   If repelling them using their ears doesn't work, apparently their noses are sensitive enough to be offended by citrus smells. Odd isn't it, that they expect us to put up with the revolting smell that they produce and yet they are offended by the zest of a lemon.

I am going to say at this point, and you may or may not believe me but it's true, that I do not find having cats and being an avid birdwatcher are a bad combination. My cats don't kill birds. They do kill mice, rats and occasionally, and sadly, shrews but for some reason – though I think this might be that I scream my head off at them if they even so much as glance at a sparrow – I find no dead birds anywhere. If you are a cat owner and a bird lover there is great advice on the RSPB website for this, too – it's really worth looking at. As for protecting my vegetable beds, I'm afraid having tried white pepper, holly and numerous other deterrents I have now resorted to permanently netting the raised beds and keeping the ground-level beds well-watered and chicken wired.

I've got it covered

Talking of netting, the added benefit of netting the beds to keep the cats off also keeps other pests away. There are so many different sorts of net available now. If pigeons are a nuisance or you are by the sea with gulls ever present, heavy duty netting is a must. Particularly if you're growing brassicas, broccoli, sprouts, cabbages and cauliflowers, this will also keep rodents away – and mice, like most of us, love peas.

Pigeons hate strong smells like cinnamon and hot peppery scents. I've seen large plastic birds of prey perched, still and lifeless, on suburban fences. I'm assuming these are to keep pigeons away and not just an aesthetic choice. I don't know if they do deter the dreaded pigeon but I know from a friend who keeps an allotment that they use a flying kite in the shape of a, wait for it, kite (or actually I think it's a peregrine falcon), fluttering above the allotments and it genuinely seems to deter at least some of the greedy old Columbae.

Netting also deals brilliantly with butterfly control – use a soft 4–7 mm (0.2–0.3 in) size mesh net – but don't do what I did and let the net touch the foliage because then they will be able to lay their eggs inside. And once they're in, they're in. Root-feeding insects are also managed well with insect-proof mesh and are better, obviously, than using pesticides. Do note that insect-pollinated crops such as strawberries and courgettes shouldn't be under insect-proof mesh during the flowering period because obviously the friendly pollinators won't be able to do their job.

Most of us nowadays are trying, in our gardening life just as in the rest of our lives, to live more sustainably and, where the gardens are concerned, organically. With this in mind, last year I started to use a biodegradable net made from plant starch. I'm hopeful that this will soon be available more widely and in a wider variety of mesh sizes because unfortunately insect-proof nylon mesh may last for up to 10 years and is not easily recycled. That said, it's always worth checking with your local recycling facilities.

If you're gardening on a smaller scale or don't want to introduce any plastic into your garden, then old-fashioned and, to my mind, beautiful, glass cloches are a must. If you're on a budget though, half-litre plastic water bottles are brilliantly recycled as a mini-cloche. Both these options have the added benefit of warming the soil and lengthening the cropping season. They also protect crops from wind damage, which, up here on a hill in rural Devon, is perfect.

Something I have to contend with here in Devon is heavy rainfall. Cloches are great at protecting delicate young foliage from the biblical storms that can hit early in the season. Do remember, though, that on hot days you should lift your cloches to get some air in and reduce the likelihood of downy mildew and other diseases that love a bit of warmth and humidity.

To be honest, if I could, I would use cloches of all sorts rather than netting just for ease of use, but unless I put each of my five cats under an individual cloche, it's a non-starter.

Glasshouse red spider mite

Lots of things are affected by this troublesome pest. In the summer it feeds on garden plants. The sap-sucking little spider causes a mottled appearance on leaves and sometimes leaf loss and plant death. House plants and greenhouse plants are affected, both ornamentals and edibles. This is a voracious little blighter. It likes vines, peaches, cucumbers, aubergines, peppers, orchids, steak and chips (*well I wouldn't put it past them*). Look out for fine, pale mottling on the upper leaf surface and on the underside, where you'll find tiny yellow-green mites, translucent white-cast skins and eggshells. You might need your reading glasses to see this properly.

Don't be fooled by the name either, these slippery little fellows don't turn red until the autumn. They might be yellowish green with two dark patches, or just to be really unhelpful they may be entirely dark the whole time. After a prolonged, heavy attack, fine silky webbing can be seen, leaves lose their colour, dry up or just fall clean off. Keep an eye open from early spring so that you can take fast action. Plants in high temperatures (my greenhouse when it's very sunny and I'm away for a little bit) need spraying with water, which will help but not control the mites. If anything in your greenhouse has a severe infestation, remove it in late summer before the shorter days trigger the females to sneak away into corners and remain dormant for the winter. If you're ever tempted to leave your greenhouse and not give it a thorough clean, this should be an incentive. Otherwise I would refer you to a biological control supplier. There are lots online or ask at your local garden centre.

Aphids, slugs and snails

The average aphid lives for about a week but a mature female can live
for 25 days, during which time she can produce 80 new aphids to add

to the gardener's misery. She doesn't even need a male partner, as Annie
Lennox told us in the 1980s – sisters can do it for themselves.

So how do we deal with this little green baby machine? I like to use
soap spray or neem oil – a regular spray stops infestation in the first

place and seems to stop them coming back. Other strong-smelling
oils are great, too. Garlic oil and water; or a few drops each of clove,

peppermint, rosemary and thyme oils mixed with water, all seem to
work well. Some people use vinegar and I hear it also works. In the
greenhouse I'm increasingly using biological controls – nematodes were

brilliant for me last year but they have to be used absolutely according
to instruction. As you've probably gathered by now, I'm a chaotic

gardener and don't always have enough time to devote to my hobby.

Slugs and snails are a nuisance in the garden but I've noticed that
the more songbirds I encourage into the veg patch, with the addition

of raised beds, the less damage I see to my plants. Besides, if you're
watching a blue tit or a robin on the bird feeder you're much less likely

to be irritated by a slimy fool taking chunks out of your courgettes.
Most of us have heard about beer traps – my son thinks that this is the

local pub but actually you sink a container into the soil and fill it with
a sweet-smelling yeasty beverage. At least they die with a happy, silly,

sluggy smile on their faces.

Other pests

Asparagus beetle

During the summer months this stunning little beetle can really ruin
your asparagus crop. I've only ever found a couple in my asparagus bed,

where I've simply picked them off by hand, examined them carefully
and found them to be totally beautiful, then dispatched them.

Caterpillars

Bruce Springsteen may have been born to run, but caterpillars have been born to eat. Encourage birds and amphibians into your garden and you shouldn't have too much trouble. If you do, however, feel the need to deal with them, it's worth learning to identify the good guys from the bad guys. If I'm really worried, I grab my mobile phone and do a paparazzi number on them, catching them from every angle and then identifying them using books or the internet. Some of them have their own Facebook pages and Instagram accounts.

Rotating veg beds

This all sounds quite depressing, but honestly, if you catch things early most things are manageable. It's so easy to say and so difficult to do when life is busy, but well-watered, well-fed plants with a little protection from predatory bugs and beetles will continue to thrive. It can also really be worth observing a crop-rotational way of growing things. This sounds complicated but in reality it just means growing different groups of vegetables in a different part of the vegetable garden each year, therefore avoiding a build-up of diseases and pest infestations. It also means that the soil is given a chance to recover from feeding one particular group of vegetables. Here is my plan:

1   Brassicas – sprouts, cauliflowers, kale
2   Legumes – peas, beans and runners
3   Alliums – onions, garlic, shallots and leeks
4   Potatoes – with the addition of tomatoes
5   Root crops – carrots, celery, parsnip

Move each section a step forward every year. If I'm going to be brutally honest with you, I have never managed to completely observe this way of growing things but I seem to be able (either by taking photographs, taking notes or simply by remembering a particularly splendid row of leeks) to recall vaguely what was where last year and often the year before. I also enjoy growing mixed beds of fruit, veg and flowers and feel that this, too, stops specific pests and diseases moving into a bed and creating a permanent home for themselves. If you are a more organised and frankly better gardener than I am, you will soon get the hang of crop rotation and I imagine a less-chaotic individual than I will embrace it and thoroughly enjoy it.

Companion planting

Here is a very simple, totally non-comprehensive guide to companion planting. As an amateur gardener these are some simple ones that I use because I find them easy to remember.

Basil

Repels spider mites and aphids. Plant it with tomatoes, peppers and lettuce. I like to eat it with all these things so it's easy to remember.

Chives

Said to deter carrot fly because of the smell. I always plant it in a row next to my carrots and remember this combination by recalling a big plate of hot, buttered carrots with little emerald circles of chives sprinkled over the top.

Parsley

Attracts beneficial insects such as damselflies. Apparently, it's particularly good near asparagus and tomatoes.

Sage

I plant a few small clumps at the edges of some of my raised beds. It has such a strong scent that I honestly believe it keeps away a lot of nameless beasties.

Thyme

Next year I'm going to plant this in my strawberry bed. I've never tried it but I hear it's a great companion and, apart from anything else, it's just one of my favourite plants in any site.

Garlic

This is apparently great to grow near roses and raspberries. Wherever I plant my garlic it just happens to be near my roses and they do seem to be good companions as I quite often hear 'Zéphirine Drouhin' (rose) chatting to 'Maddock Wight' (garlic) long into the night, clearly getting on like a house on fire.

Marigolds and nasturtiums

Before I sign off on this totally incomplete list of companion plants, I must mention marigolds and nasturtiums. I can see no earthly reason why we wouldn't plant these beautiful, bright, delightfully sunny flowers at every opportunity. They are famously good at keeping away some very nasty beetles and flies and bugs and, even if they weren't, they are both edible and a welcome sight on a sunny or dull day in any garden.

CHAPTER 8

Childhood

'Fairy tales do not tell children the dragons exist.
Children already know that dragons exist.
Fairy tales tell children the dragons can be killed.'

G.K. CHESTERTON (1874–1936)

Fairy tales are part of every culture on earth. These stories are designed to be enjoyable, but they also serve a purpose. Psychoanalysts have had a lot to say about fairy tales. Sigmund Freud suggested that they are especially helpful because, like our dreams, they express conflicts, fears and desires that we might otherwise repress. Carl Jung, too, thought that fairy tales play an essential role in allowing children a wider understanding of human nature. They offer a 'safe space', I guess, within which we can explore a scary and baffling adult world. This all makes good sense to me but something that I've noticed that I don't think the fathers of psychoanalysis talk about, is how wonderfully informative fairy tales are about plants, animals and the natural world.

The story Thumbelina literally starts with a barleycorn seed. Then we have Jack and his beanstalk (clue in the title), Cinders and her pumpkin, Beauty taking a rose from the Beast's garden. Little Red Riding Hood, one minute filling a basket with wildflowers, the next filling a wolf's belly. I don't see Rapunzel as a story about hair. For me it's about a veg plot. Rapunzel's pregnant mum, in need of a few vitamins, sends her husband to steal some salad from their neighbour's garden. Unfortunately, this neighbour is the original neighbour from hell, a sorceress. Chaos ensues and the as-yet-unborn Rapunzel is promised to the sorceress as recompense for a fistful of endive. Most gardeners are happy to share their excess produce, but always ask. You really don't want to end up swapping a beloved tabby for a courgette.

As a child I loved my illustrated books of Grimm's fairy tales and Hans Christian Andersen stories. Perhaps they are responsible for my interest in gardening, drawing and random acts of evil. I've also noticed that some of my favourite stories are a little outdated in their views on love, marriage and happy-ever-afters. So I've had a bit of fun rewriting them!

Cinderella

On the death of her mother, Cinderella's father remarried on the rebound. Worth a few quid, lonely and a bit of a softie, he was soon snapped up by a widow with two adult daughters of her own. Without being cynical and basing my judgement of her on her desperate and undignified behaviour regarding the royal family's invitation to a ball, I'd suggest that there are two ways of looking at the behaviour of Cinderella's stepmother, either she was an old-fashioned gold-digger or, more generously, a hard-up single mum doing her best for her fatherless kids.

The local prince is looking for a girl to marry – we never hear much about the gay princes, do we? Some things never change. A ball is announced so that the prince can cast his eye over the local crumpet who, it all seems, are like social climbers throughout history, gagging to marry money and a title – as I say, some things never change. It's made pretty clear to Cinders that her new fam doesn't want her to go to the cattle market – sorry – ball, and anyhow, Cinders, like Morrisey in the 1980s, hasn't got a stitch to wear.

On the night of the party, Cinderella watches her dad, his new wife and her stepsisters head off to the royal knees-up. Feeling pretty low and just about to reach for the gin bottle, a fairy godmother appears. She asks Cinderella to fetch a pumpkin from the veg patch so that she can turn it into a coach. (One hot summer I took a 45-seater coach from London to Birmingham and the air con wasn't working. Frankly, I'd rather miss a ball than do that again.) After a brief magic spell involving mice, toads, high fashion and the wave of a wand, Cinders climbs aboard the pumpkin/coach and skedaddles to the Royal Palace. As all good gardeners know, to grow well, pumpkins need plenty of sun and they don't like cold winds. Unfortunately, Cinders lived on a shady hill where the temperatures rarely rose above six degrees, so the only cucurbit she could find was a very poor specimen. Due to the clocks going back and the end of BST, there was a mix-up and

Cinderella thought it was midnight and the prince thought it was
1 a.m. Cinderella dashed off for fear of being outed as a gatecrasher,
leaving behind a single Jimmy Choo. Luckily, the prince didn't want to
escort her home in the pumpkin/coach because, as I've already said, it
was tiny, and a little bit of a squash.

When she got home, it was very late. Cinders was tired and the
champagne was wearing off. Finally she lost her temper and addressed a
few issues with her family. She told her super-controlling stepmother and
her passive-aggressive stepsisters a few home truths. Cinders reminded
her father that he'd totally failed her by allowing his new wife to treat her
as a skivvy and showed her dad the door. The women opened a bottle of
prosecco and decided that the prince wasn't all that and that they should
take care of each other and not rely on the patriarchy for approval. They
divvied up the household chores, which allowed them to spend more
time together in the vegetable patch. With dirt under their nails and
trowel in hand, they all found that gardening was their one true love
and lived happily ever after in a vegan women's collective.

Facts
Pumpkins are a type of squash. There is no botanical term 'pumpkin'.
It's just a word used by gardeners for large orange squashes that
have become very popular at Halloween. Pumpkins are part of the
Cucurbitaceae family that encompasses over 800 species of plants
known collectively as gourds or cucurbits. These include cucumbers,
melons, watermelons, pumpkins, squash and many others.

Snow White
Snow White, while in hiding from her wicked stepmother (for anyone
under 20, wicked is a bad thing in this instance), opened the door to
a little old lady proffering a basket of apples. Not recognising the old
crone as her wicked stepmother, Snow White agreed to share an apple
with the old woman, who sliced the apple in half and ate the green side.

Snow White, having eaten the red side, fell into a narcoleptic coma. The seven little guys who had given her board and lodging in return for cooking, cleaning and the weekly laundering of eight sets of bed linen, believed her dead. They were inconsolable. Good housekeepers are hard to come by, especially in rural locations, and this girl was a dream. Not only did she keep the place ship-shape and sing to rabbits and roe deer but she managed to get on with all the guys, even the trickier personalities. Never a fan of the chinstrap beard, Snow White kept her thoughts to herself even though it was clear to her that Grumpy was a misogynist and Doc had never done a day at medical college.

Devastated at the loss of the domestic help, upon her death they put Snow White in a glass coffin. (I've no idea why they opted for glass. It seems an impractical and rather ghoulish choice but perhaps it was an homage to her extraordinary window-cleaning skills.) It was placed outside the cottage so that the creatures of the forest could come and pay their respects. A prince happened to be riding by, probably on his way to a polo match and, seeing a huddle of hares, foxes, stags and guys in red and green jackets, thought he'd stumbled on a hunt ball.

When he heard the story of Snow White, the princess in hiding, he offered to take her coffin to the palace and to her father, the king.

On the long journey back, the cart bearing the glass coffin hit a pothole. The jolt dislodged the piece of poisoned apple from Snow White's throat, and she awoke. (Given the appalling state of the country roads in Devon where I live, I find this part of the story entirely believable.)

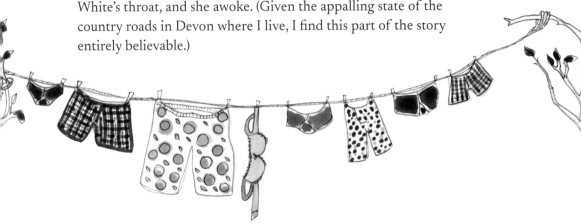

As you'd expect, Snow White marries the prince, whether out of love or gratitude, we're not told. Either way, without a cleaner, the cottage in the woods soon descended into chaos again and featured on an episode of *The World's Worst Hoarders*, and for the first time in history an entire highway maintenance team were in the New Year's Honours List for shoddy workmanship.

Moral(s)
Both red and green apples are delicious but green are better for you. They have twice as much vitamin A.

Or: *life is like a road – there will be bumps along the way.*

Facts
Some people are sensitive to chemicals called salicylates that occur naturally in apples and may cause swelling and rashes. I've often wondered if the wicked stepmother has been wrongly accused of murderous intent and that in fact Snow White just had a nasty allergic reaction to the fruit.

For most of us, though, apples are a very healthy choice, being packed with antioxidants and fibre, vitamin C and potassium. Recent research by the *European Journal of Nutrition* found that eating pectin-rich whole apples lowers cholesterol, particularly in post-menopausal woman (she said with a mouthful of Braeburn). They are also low GI, so might improve insulin sensitivity and may help prevent diabetes.

There are also ongoing studies that suggest apples may help the gut microbiome, inflammatory disorders, bone and heart health. They are so nutritious an apple a day may well help to keep the doctor away.

Sleeping Beauty
Yet another furious witch at the bottom of this one. Honestly, the menopause is so little understood in these stories.

Having been 'accidentally' left off the christening invitation list, the 'bad' fairy curses the baby princess Aurora, stating that on the girl's 16th birthday she will fall asleep for 100 years. After some ill-advised crafting at a spinning wheel this does indeed happen. The entire palace staff take the opportunity for a well-earned kip, too, until eventually a prince slashes his way through a century's worth of brambles to wake Aurora from her sleep. Anyone who has ever tried to clear brambles with a machete (or a sword) will know that by the time he'd reached her and given her a big kiss, the brambles would have grown back twice as thick behind him. The loved-up pair would have had to hire professional land-clearing teams to get them out or they'd be there still, their pretty faces covered in bloody scratches and nettle stings, begging for loppers and leather pruning gloves.

Brambles

Like most gardeners, I loathe brambles. They are a pain and can take over a piece of land devastatingly quickly, but I do love the word! It just suits them so well. Brambles are prickly shrubs of the rose family, including raspberries and blackberries, wild roses and thorns.

On my wedding day to Sam, he presented me with five adorable piglets. They grew quickly and I soon discovered that pigs are the best way to clear ground of brambles. Pigs will happily, very happily, snout out bramble roots, up to a foot or more below the soil's surface. Watching them enjoy their work is fantastic. They look excited, as happy as pigs in s . . . oil! Perhaps pigs aren't the best solution for an urban garden though. I'm afraid with most plots it's a case of donning protective gear. Take care of your eyes too, as the thick thorny stems tend to spring back and hit you in the face. Cut back as much as you can and then dig out the roots. Try to clear every last trace though, as any sections of root left will be back to take over again in the time it takes to ask: 'What's the osteopath's number?'

Thumbelina

This has always been a favourite with me because in this story Hans
Christian Andersen really reveals his fascination with the natural world.
This is my take on it but I've tried to keep his references to plants and
animals intact because this fairy tale is a brilliant introduction to the
wonders of nature, and it encouraged me as a child to observe the
countryside around me with a better understanding.

Once upon a time a childless couple bought a barleycorn seed from a
passing witch, for a shilling. One seed for one shilling – that is one very
pricey seed, but they weren't hoping for a sweet pea or a sunflower, or
even a sheaf of barley, which is presumably what you'd normally get
from a barleycorn seed. They were expecting great things from their
little seed – a much-longed-for baby. I love babies but even allowing for
inflation, it's a lot of money to hand over for a single seed that might, as
all gardeners know, fail to germinate.

Happily, for the couple in the story, this little seed does germinate
and produces a beautiful flower. When the would-be parents peel back
the petals, inside the flower, lying on a cushion of golden stamen, is
a tiny baby girl. The baby is so small that they call her Thumbelina
because she is just the size of her father's thumb. As Thumbelina grows
up she is everything the couple have so longed for, only presumably,
smaller. They adore her and she them. She's kind and loving and
generally a smashing daughter.

Unfortunately, from here on in things aren't so straightforward. Life
gets pretty traumatic for Thumbelina. One night as she is snoozing
in her walnut-shell bed, snuggled up under a tulip-petal bedcover, a
mummy toad (*Bufo bufo*) kidnaps her, intending to marry her off to
her singleton son. (I can only assume that dating apps weren't up to
much back then and that her warty boy was struggling to find love.
Toads always get a bad press and this story doesn't do much for their
PR.) Despite Thumbelina's tears and protestations, mummy toad is
determined that a wedding will take place. If you've ever seen a toad eat

a slug, you'll understand why Thumbelina wasn't keen to sit opposite toad boy at a wedding breakfast.

While awaiting the nuptials, Thumbelina is left alone for a moment, stranded on a waterlily pad (*Nymphaeaceae*). Her falling tears attract the attention of a passing fish that feels sorry for her and gnaws away at the stem of the water lily, freeing it to float quickly downstream, taking our little heroine away from her warty captors. She ties a white butterfly to her water-lily leaf and it acts as a sail, making her journey even faster. (In my garden white butterflies tend to be cabbage whites and would certainly eat her boat, leaving nothing but a stumpy stalk.) After a brief moment of joy, sailing downstream, inevitably things take a turn. The poor kid, having escaped the toad, has a further series of ghastly suitors.

They include a cockchafer, which you may know as a maybug and is not a looker (particularly in the larvae stage), and an elderly, cantankerous field mouse that persuades her to get engaged to his mate, a mole. The mole insists that when they marry, Thumbelina will have to see out the rest of her days underground and out of the sunshine. This is definitely a case of coercive control.

Luckily, Thumbelina meets a swallow that is exhausted by a long flight from sunnier climes (probably too many G-and-Ts and jet lag, if my experience is anything to go by). Anyhow, she rehydrates him and together they fly away from the ghastly string of blokes she's run into and she eventually gets married to a tiny prince. This is deemed a happy ending, but given the dubious behaviour of some modern-day princes, I'd probably advise her to go for the toad.

Jack and the Beanstalk

Jack sold his cow for a handful of beans and the rest is history.

Peter Rabbit

Thinking back to my own childhood and to that of my children, there are so many wonderful stories of gardens and gardening. Mr McGregor in Beatrix Potter's *The Tale of Peter Rabbit* is probably most people's introduction to literary depictions of gardeners and he's not a sympathetic figure. Murderous, always furious at being outwitted, unhealthily red in the face as his carrots come under siege from Ma Rabbit's fluffy little gang of hoodlums, Flopsy, Mopsy and Baby Face AKA Cotton Tail and their leader, Peter.

As children we are encouraged to be charmed by Peter. Yet his dapper blue jacket and shiny brass buttons disguise his true nature. As a keen vegetable gardener, myself, I put it to you, dear reader, that it is time to view the actions of one Mr P. Rabbit in a different light. I suggest that we have been led, quite literally up the garden path, by this career criminal. A repeat offender, that, despite countless warnings

that he would end up inside a pie, continued in his perfidious activities, showing no remorse for his victim, a helpless pensioner with high blood pressure. It has been suggested that because the accused's father was shot in cold blood by Mr McGregor and turned into pie filling that Peter is merely seeking gangland-style revenge in this hideous turf war – he merely is reclaiming his patch, so to speak. I suggest, therefore, that there be a firearms amnesty and that if Mr McGregor agrees to lead a totally vegetarian life and that Peter grow his own bloody carrots, peace may be restored and everything in the veg garden will be lovely once again.

Adam and Eve

Garden of Eden. So far so good. God tells Eve: 'Eat any fruit you want *except* that Apple.' I mean, she didn't stand a *chance*.

Alice in Wonderland

Alice eats an unidentified mushroom in this story, which explains a lot. The psilocybin mushroom, more commonly known as the magic mushroom, is known to contain a hallucinogen which makes one feel paranoid, anxious, confused and overwhelmed. Poor Alice, no wonder she was baffled when she came across people painting white roses red to keep the Queen happy! But then again, I've known of many garden designers who have got up to all sorts of tricks at the Chelsea Flower Show the day before the royal visit.

A baby that turns into a pig, a caterpillar smoking dope and a cat up a tree. In this story, the last remnant of the cat is a smile; unlike my cats who leave less pleasant reminders of their visits.

CHAPTER 9

Herbs

'There's rosemary, that's for remembrance;
pray, love, remember...'

OPHELIA IN *HAMLET* BY WILLIAM SHAKESPEARE
(1564–1616)

Where do I start when it comes to talking about the importance of herbs in the garden and in my life? I'm not going to include every herb here. I'm just going to tell you about my relationship with some of my favourites – the ones that I plant annually because I really can't imagine living without them, in the kitchen, in the medicine cabinet and in the flower border. Some of them, in fact most of them, not only look wonderful growing into beautiful specimen plants but are useful in so many different ways.

So what's a herb? It might sound silly to those of us who regularly grab a handful of dried oregano to enhance a Greek salad or pop a bay leaf into a stew or gravy but sometimes, just as it's hard to tell the wood from the trees, it's hard to tell a herb from any other plant.

Herbs, herbalists and the use of nature as a medicine cabinet have really come back into focus in recent years.

One dictionary description of a herb is: 'A plant that does not develop persistent woody tissue but dies down at the end of a growing season.' This seems to me to be saying that bay is not a herb, and I suppose it is probably classed as a tree, but in my house a bay leaf is very much in the herb section of the larder. Another dictionary description is: 'A plant or plant part valued for its medicinal, savoury or aromatic qualities.' Which, again, doesn't seem to fully do justice to the herbs I have in my garden, making no mention of the utterly delightful ways in which herbs can add to the beauty of a flower border or kitchen garden and the way they can be used to perfume our homes.

I love to scent my bath water with a big bunch of rosemary, lavender or dried thyme, simply tied with a piece of string or ribbon and dangled under a running tap, then left hanging in the warm water to scent it as I bathe. What's brilliant about this is that you get all the delight of the perfume of the plant but it also releases some of the wonderful oils that are so good for our skin and so relaxing to breathe in while we take a soak.

Herbs, herbalists and the use of nature as a medicine cabinet have really come back into focus in recent years. We gardeners, even if we have very little space and just pots to grow in or windowsills to grow on, can access these wonderful plants easily. It's worth noting that most herbs need cutting back regularly to keep them in good shape, therefore the more you use the longer your plant will keep producing and the longer you can prevent them going to seed.

Bay leaves

Whenever I smell a bay leaf, I am immediately taken back to Christmas mornings over the years. The aromatic smell of a bay leaf infusing turkey gravy fills me with happiness. It speaks of family, feast, friends and the traditions of festive gatherings. In British culture, bay leaves tend to be used mostly at Christmas, which, given the versatility and the accessibility of the bay leaf, is slightly absurd. Just thinking about Indian cuisine for instance, makes me realise that I underuse and underestimate this wonderful herb.

I think, like lots of home cooks, I use them in any dish that is cooked slowly – stews, soups, pasta sauces – and they do work brilliantly used in this way. Use only a couple of leaves per dish since the aromatic nature of bay means that a little goes a long way.

Talking of Christmas and bay leaves, because I have access to plenty of leaves and because it costs me nothing and they dry quickly, in early December I like to string them together on a piece of thick cotton or twine, interspersing them with holly or hawthorn berries (fake ones if the birds have eaten the real ones). Depending on what sort of decorations I'm having that year, I'll either leave them in their natural earthy colours and make a wreath or a garland for the stairs or, occasionally, if I'm having a really camp, showbiz Christmas, I will end up spraying them with gold or silver paint and covering them in lashings of glitter, even twisting in little baubles that will catch the light and make a real statement. What can I say? You can take the girl out of the theatre but you can't take the theatre out of the girl, especially at Christmas.

Just getting back to the kitchen for a minute and the use of bay for its flavour and fragrance in many Indian dishes such as biryani and curries, I think it's also worth mentioning the purported medical and health benefits of the bay leaf.

On the advice of a friend, I've started to infuse water with bay leaves as a home remedy for migraine. I have no idea whether or not it's of any real benefit but I find it immensely comforting and it can also help relieve any gastric problems I may be having (which is a fairly common occurrence because I have coeliac disease). I've also heard that it's useful in soothing irritable bowel syndrome. With any of these ailments I'm of the opinion that as long as you do it safely and carefully it's worth a go. With this in mind, here's a little recipe:

Bay leaf tea/tisane
2–3 bay leaves | water

1 Cut bay leaves (wash them first, if needed) into smallish pieces.
2 Add to boiling water.
3 Soak overnight.
4 Strain the water the following day.
5 Drink first thing in the morning and throughout the day.

Growing bay trees (*Laurus nobilis*) does require a little space. It's always a popular choice, whether you have patio or a bigger garden. If, unlike me, you keep them neatly clipped, two simple bay trees can make a brilliant statement at the entrance of a house or at the start of a pathway. If left to grow a little wilder and untamed, they form big, dark glossy plants that will fill the back of a border, with what I consider to be a real presence, a strong sculptural statement. What I have done with some of mine, in the border when they get too big, is to take out the bottom branches, creating a longer stem or trunk, and then I can shape the top in any way I fancy. If I don't like it, I trim it gently over a few seasons so that, like a hairstyle, I can grow it out and change it! During winter I love coming home to what looks like a sort of cast of characters in the garden. Large bay trees are a big, powerful presence waiting to greet me just as the light fades. I trust these guys, they're stalwarts. I get an overwhelming sense of calm and permanence when I look at my bay trees, so whether you're going to clip a single patio specimen into a neat little ball or create a series of gigantic magical shapes – peacocks and pyramids as far as the eye can see – go for it. Living with a bay tree gives every day a lift. Just a reminder that they don't like the cold, particularly when they are in pots, so raise the pot and wrap it up snuggly if the days are looking cold and damp.

Chives

From majestic bay trees to tiny, delicate chives. One of the easiest herbs to propagate, chives are a beginner's herb. Sprinkle a few seeds on some damp compost, keep damp for a few days, then pop a plastic bag (or something that creates a mini-propagator) over the pot and before you know it you will start cutting from these tasty onion-flavoured beauties. In the garden they will self-seed and soon, with any luck, you'll have banks of the purplish-pink punky little flowers brightening up wherever they decide to settle. This Toyah Wilcox of the herb family is always welcome in any soup or on any salad.

Parsley

There are lots of superstitions about parsley.

'Plant parsley ... get pregnant.' *True.* I did in 1999 and I did get pregnant. *False.* I did in 2020 (post-menopause), and – not pregnant – odd!

'Parsley grows where the woman of the household is in charge.' *True.* (Don't ask me how I know – ask Sam.)

'Parsley is in league with the devil!' (No proof.) It takes so long to emerge from the ground it was thought that its roots extended down to the very pits of hell. The only way to protect yourself from old Nick was to plant it at 3 p.m. on Good Friday which, for Christians, is the time of Jesus' crucifixion. In some villages they didn't dare touch the seeds but would blow them onto the soil from the top of a bible.

Pouring boiling water onto parsley seeds was also recommended and still is in some quarters; presumably it's supposed to help germination by warming the soil. (*Don't know*).

During winter I love coming home to what looks like a sort of cast of characters in the garden.

I grow both curly and flat-leafed parsley. I love the flavour and, because it has such a long season, seeing us right through from late spring into late autumn, it's wonderful for spring recipes and summer dishes alike: asparagus risotto and warming autumnal soups and fish pies. Because it grows in abundance here, I'll often make batches of parsley butter and freeze them so I can simply stir it into dishes that need perking up.

Parsley is incredibly nutritious – two tablespoons will provide 12 per cent of your recommended daily allowance of vitamin A, 16 per cent of your recommended vitamin C and a whopping 154 per cent of your recommended vitamin K (vitamin K is essential for blood clotting), so it's great for immunity, your bones and heart health.

Thyme

This darling, compact, evergreen shrub grows easily in a warm, sunny spot. Thyme, closely related to oregano, is anti-bacterial, anti-fungal, drought tolerant and, once you've got it, you don't need to do anything with it. My ideal herb. There are so many varieties, scents and colours, each producing clusters of tiny pink, mauve or white flowers, all so rich in nectar the pollinating insects go crazy for it. This is what to grow if you want to show bees a really good thyme.

I've grown lots of different varieties on a sloping border, the subtle differences in colour and form create a beautiful puffy quilt that is always covered in bees when in flower. Thyme is a key ingredient in a bouquet garni. Sow it in the spring somewhere nice and warm and you should see signs of life within a couple of weeks.

It's hard to think of a dish that isn't improved by using thyme. It's great with roasted vegetables and to create a rub for all sorts of meat dishes. Also beautiful with roasted asparagus and I have to admit to having enjoyed a cocktail recently in the south of France (no less), where the bartender had singed a sprig of thyme and popped it into a . . . actually I can't remember what the cocktail was now, I think I must have had two, or three?

Oregano

I associate oregano, which I grow in abundance here in Devon, with mainly two things. Firstly, Greek dishes – in classical Greek the name means 'joy of the mountain'; the Greeks also call it wild marjoram. When dried the flavour is more intense – they say good-quality oregano numbs the tongue.

The other association I have with oregano – and please look away now if you are squeamish – is when I make an anti-fungal poultice for any nail infections . . .

Poultice
1 garlic clove | 1 tbsp oregano | 1 tbsp olive oil | 6 sage leaves

1   Put it all in a blender and give it a whizz.
2   Pack it onto the affected area, putting your feet or your hands into a plastic bag (I sometimes put cotton wool in to keep it in contact with the affected nails) and then lie back and think of Mykonos. *I'm really not joking, if you do this regularly it works better than anything I've bought over the counter.*
3   Keep the batch in the fridge and repeat the process every day. *You'll get some funny looks if you go to the supermarket in flip flops as the smell is pungent. Here in rural Devon, it's one of the nicer smells you meet on the street.*

Rosemary
The quickest way to propagate rosemary is by taking cuttings in mid-May or June.

1   Select a healthy plant with lots of new growth and, using a sharp knife, take a 7.5-cm (3-in) cutting from young shoots just below a leaf joint (or I just tear them off a stem).
2   Put 5 cm (2 in) of bare stem into a glass of water and change the water every week.
3   After two weeks you should see roots emerging.
4   Transplant into potting compost and grow on.

Rosemary has such an intense flavour that, although I love it, I tend to use it quite sparingly. It's brilliant with garlic and added to roast potatoes. A sprig in baked camembert elevates the dish from a lovely snack to a gourmet feast.

Coriander

So many people hate coriander, I almost feel that just writing the word will get me cancelled but I'm 62 years old and, frankly, if being cancelled means a bit of peace and quiet, then, CORIANDER.

I love it.

Sow outdoors or indoors for an earlier crop, obviously. They make a pretty sexy micro-green, packing in a lot of flavour for a very small amount of leaf. Scatter the seeds in shallow drills or on the surface of firmed compost in containers, cover with a little soil or compost, and water. Germination will happen in three weeks. If you don't like coriander, and there *is* a genuine physiological difference between those who do and those who don't, there is a Japanese herb called mitsuba that is similar – at least I think it's a herb. It might be a hatchback.

Mint

Just grow mint because you would be foolish not to. It is the scent and flavour of summer. Be warned though, it's a bugger for taking over a herb patch or any part of the garden. I grow it in a bucket and then sink the bucket below the surface of the soil by about 7.5 cm (3 in). Partial shade is best as it's prone to flowering and going to seed. Best advice – cut big handfuls of it, as the younger leaves are much tastier and it keeps it under control.

Don't grow mint near other herbs if you can avoid it as it's a terrible nutrient thief. On the other hand the scent of mint repels aphids, flea beetles, whiteflies and apparently rats aren't keen on a minty whiff.

The menthol irritates their nasal cavities, which, as a rat hater, really makes me laugh. The idea of them sneezing their ratty way out of my vegetable patch delights me.

Lemon balm

I grow lemon balm to make a soothing drink. Just steep a large cutting, about the size of your hand, in hot water and, when it's infused, sip it for anything that ails you. A handful in a hot bath is great if you are flagging before a party or social event. It's so easy to grow from seed unless you want a named variety.

Melissa officinalis, AKA bee balm, is a hardy perennial great for ground cover, cottage gardens, wildlife gardens and lazy gardeners like me because it looks so beautiful and healthy with a regime of absolutely nothing ... while taking regular cuttings.

Borage

This is also known as star flower. I use this mostly as a garnish for Pimm's or to decorate cocktails or salads. The Persians call it cow's tongue flower. I think I'll stick with borage. It's thought to be good for companion planting with spinach, brassicas and beans. Apparently brilliant to companion plant with tomatoes, too, which I can't attest to yet (I'm trying it for the first time this year) but like everything, it's worth a go.

The beautiful sky blue, pale-pink or white flowers have a cucumber-like fragrance. It's an annual, so plant each year or let it self-seed. It's super easy to grow and I think it's incredibly romantic to look at. On a summer evening when the bees, which love blue flowers, are gently buzzing from flower to flower, I think it's truly a perfect plant, bringing the ideal combinations of scent, sound and vision into the garden.

Of course, there are hundreds of herbs to grow, enjoy and use. If I had to choose only one sort of garden, I think it would be a herb garden. There is something magical about the medicinal, the perfumed and the edible all coming together in one place. Even *coriander*.

CHAPTER 10

Fluttery, prickly & wriggly chums

'The longer I live, the more beautiful life becomes.'

FRANK LLOYD WRIGHT (1867–1959)

When I was 10 years old, one of my dearest friends at school was Sarah. One spring term Sarah discovered a blue tit's nest in a dilapidated brick wall in a very old part of the school's walled gardens. The crumbling brickwork was hidden behind lots of ancient tree stumps and roots that were cloaked in dark green ivy – it was a mysterious and frightening place that smelt of decay and sap and damp earth. Needless to say, it was completely out of bounds. Sarah shared with me the joy of peering into the perfect little nest, delicate and lined with velvety green moss. On hearing our approach, the five completely bald, bulging-eyed, just-hatched baby blue tits would snap open the huge golden ovals of their beaks, mistaking two breathless 10-year-old girls for their blue-and-yellow parents, hoping that they were about to be fed. It was the only place I ever wanted to be.

I would sit through dull maths lessons gazing out of the window and dreaming, not of David Cassidy or Donny Osmond but of *Cyanistes caeruleus*, our beloved blue tits. Away at boarding school, life at home having become difficult, I was feeling isolated and lonely. Sarah and I formed a deep bond through our devotion to our secret nest. Those vulnerable babies would shake their big heads in anticipation of a juicy caterpillar meal. One baby blue tit can eat up to 150 caterpillars in a day. Female blue tits can lay up to 13 eggs in a clutch. That's a lot of caterpillars that don't make it to devastate our gardens, but I'm getting ahead of myself.

That summer term, Sarah changed my life forever. She had grown up in rural Dorset rather than in suburbia as I had – she was a country girl. She was also a member of what sounded to me like the most glamourous club in the world – it was called Young Ornithologists. I think it was part of and perhaps still is a part of the Royal Society for the Protection of Birds (RSPB). The RSPB's president was, at the time, a very famous newscaster called Robert Dougal. He was an ancient old man, probably nearly 40, with big sad eyes and a sweet smile. He'd always been my favourite newsreader and then when

I found out that he was also president of the RSPB, he became a god. The creation of the RSPB was the inspiration of three young women, Emily Williamson (née Bateson), Eliza Phillips and Etta Lemon. Sickened by the slaughter of exotic birds for their feathers for adorning high fashion hats and jackets, they started the Society for the Protection of Birds in 1891 to campaign for change. Their efforts helped bring about the 1921 Plumage (Prohibition) Act and the founding of a global force to save nature.

As a member, I received its magazine, *Bird Life*. Getting post when you're away at boarding school is a big deal (or at least it was back in the days when letter writing was compulsory on a Sunday and there was no access to the single coin-operated telephone in the upstairs hall until you were 16 and wanted to share all your private information and feelings not only with your family but with the entire fifth form). So at 10 years of age a letter from Robert Dougal telling me that the population of dunnocks was happily increasing was like a love letter from the natural world into a hollow and sometimes desolate place. Being careful never to disturb the nest or to frighten the busy blue tit parents away from their duties of feeding their young brood, Sarah and I broke the school rules as often as possible and, suffering nettle stings and scratched legs, made our way quietly to visit our little family. At the end of term, when the babies had fledged and flown and the parents moved away, Sarah and I were devastated. I was sadder still when, due to a change in family circumstances, the following term Sarah didn't return to school.

Blue tits

Blue tits are still a favourite watch for me. I have a very strong memory of watching a flock of well over 20 bathing in the rainwater that had filled the upturned cups of huge, pale-pink *Magnolia x soulangeana* flowers in a London garden that I once knew. The sunlight sparkling off the spray, flicking into the air like glass bugle beads from the damp,

shaggy, rain-sodden feathers of those beautiful twittering idiots is an
image that has never left me. When I look at my bird feeder now, here
in Devon, and I see not just blue tits but coal tits, great tits and long-tail
tits feeding happily on the hugely expensive seed I buy for them, I want
to tell them that it is because of some of their distant cockney relatives
that I'm keeping them all so well-fed today!

Talking of bird feeders, I wonder how many of us spend hours (and
I'm deliberately not saying wasted hours, as, to my mind, any time
devoted to watching birds is never wasted) just gazing at our feathered
friends. I defy anyone to give a bird table three minutes' attention, real
attention, and not be addicted to birdwatching. It is the crack cocaine
of the natural world. As I write, the UK's annual spend on bird-feeding
products ranges from £200 to £300 million. I'm not thinking of
picking up a crack pipe anytime soon but doing the maths it might
be a less costly indulgence.

With that in mind, this is a recipe for homemade bird cake that I
think works out cheaper than buying readymade fat snacks.

Bird cake

70 g (2½ oz/½ cup) good-quality bird seed | 40 g (1½ oz/¼ cup) raisins |
30 g (1 oz/¼ cup) peanuts | 20 g (¾ oz/¼ cup) grated cheese |
1 x 250 g/9 oz pack suet or lard | yoghurt pots (with hole in bottom,
string tied through and knotted), large pinecones or old coconut shells,
halved and washed | large mixing bowl | scissors

1   Bring the lard up to room temperature, cut it into chunks and
     place in a bowl.
2   Add the other ingredients, squidging it all together until it binds.
3   Fill whatever receptacle you are using. *Sometimes a big clean
     pinecone smothered in this fatty mixture looks really great and
     if you hang it on a piece of string the birds really like to dangle
     off it.*

4   Put your completed fat snacks into the fridge and a couple of
     hours later they are ready to go and feed the greedy sweethearts.
5   Feed! If a coconut or pinecone, place treats onto a flat feeding
     tray, or hang the yoghurt pots.

WARNING Don't do this with children with nut allergies. Bird seed
and bird peanuts are not suitable for human consumption. Also, dogs
and cats can be quite sick if they get access to any of this, so if you've
got a greedy labrador or similar, keep them away.

Blackbirds

In the Paul McCartney song 'Blackbird', the Eurasian blackbird you
can hear on this Beatles' track always hits me in the solar plexus.
Despite being one of the most common birds in the UK, it's hard to
take this stunning bird for granted. The male – oily black, yellow-
eyed and golden-beaked – has to be one of the most bird-looking
birds that exists. If I think of a bird, it is this chunky, well-formed,
perfectly-silhouetted shape that comes to mind and this boy can sing.
A blackbird's song, at any time of year, stops me in my tracks and I
always feel I have to honour this bird with my attention.

   The females are all together softer looking – soft browns with spots and
streaks, and their beaks are a muted beige. Female blackbirds rarely sing,
unlike life in my household where I'm glad to say the male, my husband,
rarely sings and my daughter and I warble endlessly. During the breeding
season, a female blackbird will respond vocally to the courtship of the
male. It's important for my husband to know at this point that I will never
respond to courtship singing from him unless it is to run away. Indeed at a
wedding recently, when Sam decided to give full vent to 'Love Divine, All
Loves Excelling', I poked him so hard in the ribs that he doubled over and
friends thought that he was deeply moved by the beauty of the event.

   Like Sam Farmer, blackbirds are monogamous, choosing a partner until
death they do part. When house hunting, Mr and Mrs *Turdus merula*,

like lots of us, do it together. I love the image of a pair of blackbirds hunkered over a property website, wondering whether or not they will need room for two or more eggs and a car porch. It seems that the male is very keen for his partner to feel happy and comfortable with the nesting site. These are just some of the reasons I think that garden birders like me feel so connected to the blackbird.

I love to hear them in the dawn chorus but the sound that really enters my soul is the sound I associate with late autumn and the onset of winter – the shrill and sudden accelerating almost scream and the 'chuck, chuck, chuck' that I can hear just before nightfall. I think these calls are territorial and the presence of these sounds in my life from childhood right up until today, both in the countryside and in cities, are a comforting, unchanging soundtrack in a sometimes baffling and rapidly changing world. If I'm away filming, in an unknown strange city, a blackbird sounding a bedtime alarm call settles me and allows me to connect to the happier, more rural part of my nature.

Bees

I was stung by a bee once, right underneath my thumbnail. It was excruciatingly painful but that day I was grateful to find out that I don't have a serious allergic reaction to their venom. I wish the same could be said of my feelings about television and theatre critics over the years, whose venom is still ouchy. I'm not keen on critics but I do love bees and I am a forgiving woman. Once I'd taken an antihistamine tablet, I was ready to kiss and make up with my red-bottomed attacker. The red-tailed bumble bee is a very large black bee with a bright red rear end. It's prolific in the UK, in gardens, farmland and hedgerows and anywhere there are plenty of flowers to feed on.

Planting for bees, even in a small garden, is easy and immensely gratifying. Single flowers are best, as double flowers make it tricky for bees to get to the central part of the flower. Single-flowered dahlias like 'Happy Days' or 'Single Kiss Purple', as well as blue flowers, are favourites for them as they see purple more clearly than any other colour. That said, bees really will be grateful for flowers of any colour. I find in my own garden that they particularly love what I think of as cottage-garden plants: foxgloves, snapdragons, honeysuckle and penstemons. In a more established garden you'll notice them guzzling on hawthorn, crab apple, rosemary and, in the late summer, buddleia, single-flowered dahlias and, don't forget, ivy. Although the tiny green flowers of ivy don't impress me much, they are hugely attractive to pollinating insects such as hoverflies, honey bees and butterflies. Ivy offers a huge amount of pollen and nectar and, because of its upright habit, it can offer a plentiful supply of food while taking up very little space on a patio or in a tiny urban garden.

Bees, wasps, bumbles

Early in the year, really from March onwards (the clue is in the name), you'll spot the early bumble bee. It is the UK's smallest. As a gardener I love it because it plays such an important part in pollinating our summer fruits. When I'm picking my first crop of raspberries, I always think of the early bumble bees that I see keeping so busy in the first few warm days of spring and summer.

Who likes wasps? Other wasps? Not many of us are keen to invite them to picnics or outdoor lunches or welcome them into our houses. Who likes honey bees? Everybody likes honey bees. But how many of us can tell the difference between a wasp and a honey bee? Not enough of us apparently. They do have a similar shape – both slender with narrow waists and hips, like Harry Styles – but this is where the similarities end. Wasps are very clearly bright yellow with deep black bands around their abdomen, bees are more the colour of soft brown sugar and dark brown sugar, and there is only one species of honey bee in the UK.

Bees have been domesticated for centuries. In the wild they live in wooded areas in large hives made of wax honeycombs. Every year a new queen lays eggs while the workers look after the young. Butterflies, moths and other insects pollinate many of our crops but bees do the lion's share of the pollinating work and have a crucial role to play. Many crops worldwide are best pollinated by animals, and bees are the best. This may not be the first thing to come to mind when I'm quietly sitting in the garden at the end of a warm summer day listening to the lazy buzzing of a bumble bee, drunk on pollen, fat as Falstaff and as unperturbed by my presence. I know how hard he's been working all day to feed his queen and I like to think he knows that some of my hard work in the garden is for his benefit.

I plant to please the bees. I adopted No Mow May, the national campaign launched by the botanical charity Plantlife in 2019. Most of us were very happy to join in with a movement that encourages us to delay mowing the lawn and to allow nectar-filled flowers to thrive so that bees, butterflies and moths get an early supply of energy. Since I took Plantlife's advice a couple of years ago I have totally embraced the concept. I now think of my gardening life as No Mow No More. I very rarely cut the grass and, on bigger pieces of land, have let wild grasses take over. The abundance of wildflowers, butterflies and moths is staggering and has completely altered the landscape here in just a few years. I find it intensely moving to be

taken back to a natural landscape that reminds me more of my childhood, when less of our land was drenched in pesticides. It's so good to see white clover, red clover, self heal and oxeye daisies with clouds of brimstone, gatekeeper and marbled white butterflies dancing above the native plants when I walk the dogs, the mother-of-pearl sky above me and the sound of the warm breeze rustling the grasses beneath my feet.

Just after finishing the last paragraph about bees and butterflies, and I swear this is true, a honey bee flew in the window of the room where I am writing and landed on the watercolour of some flowers that I have been drawing. It just landed lightly, buzzed a few times, genuinely appeared to look me in the eye and left. I have been feeling quite low the last few days, and maybe it's just my imagination (as I say I've not been feeling entirely myself lately), but it felt like a sort of much needed thank you.

Three beautiful birds

Time moves more quickly these days but I am still grateful for winter's end and the beginning of spring. It's a cliche I know but the first returning swallows, and some years there are piteously few, lift my spirits like nothing else. Although the first to arrive are usually in southern England, others head north as they are very focused on flying directly to their favourite nesting sites. Weather conditions play a huge part in where and when the birds make landfall. We know, too, that climate change is altering arrival dates. Swifts and house martins are now on the International Union for the Conservation of Nature (IUCN) Red List of Threatened Species for UK birds, but so are more familiar birds like house sparrows and starlings, which have recently suffered huge declines. As of 2021 there are now 70 species on the Red List. Conservation efforts do make a real difference and this is where we gardeners can really help.

With swifts and house martins in real trouble, you can help them hugely by putting up nest boxes. They need three things to breed successfully: somewhere to build a home, the materials to build it with and a food source. They only eat insects that they catch on the wing so, unless you are part of a trapeze act with access to huge amounts of greenfly, you can't help them in the air or by putting out the usual bird food as you would for other species. Bodies of water, even small ones, are ideal for encouraging a sort of airborne insect buffet. They love mosquitoes and devour them in huge numbers. To watch them skimming over the pond here at the farm on a summer evening is delightful; their skill in flight is breathtaking. Sometimes when I'm swimming they come so close to my head that I swear if I had nits they'd have a snack. Their nests are made solely from mud and, just like Peppa Pig, they love a muddy puddle. You can also put up nest cups, which mimic the goblet shape of their home-built nests, but don't be offended if they ignore them for the first year. They like to live in colonies and might be nervous of setting up home in isolation, but it is thought that just seeing a new home may encourage them to form a community the following year.

It's easy to confuse swifts, house martins and swallows, which is odd because swifts are unrelated to house martins and swallows. I think of them as a group though, mostly because of the way they fill the skies and because of their extraordinary aerodynamic shapes. Swifts are actually a very dark chocolatey brown but appear black against the sky. They have a pale throat but move so fast it's hard to spot. Some visitors here spend the rest of the year in sub-Saharan Africa. Swifts spend their entire life in the air with the exception of a brief breeding season – even these aeronautical geniuses take a break for love.

House martins are absurdly cute – rounder with blue, black and white feathers. In flight, they are a stiff-winged bird with a jerky flying action. If you're unsure though as to what you're looking at, a white rump will clinch it – it's a house martin.

Swallows are a delicate, dark, glossy blue-black with red throats, pale underside and two long tail streamers. They are the most agile in flight. According to Shakespeare, Cervantes, Marlow and John Dunn, comparisons are odious – or odorous (in other words, they stink) – but it's hard not to compare these three stunning summer visitors. I'm not prepared to pick a favourite though. OK, swifts.

The rough with the smooth
Even here in Devon, where our nearest neighbours are both working farms and there is very little in the way of traffic, it's very rare for me to see a live hedgehog. An increasing loss of hedgerows, changes in farming practices and because they don't have access to social media,

means that simply meeting other hedgehogs is harder than it used to be. The safe tracks and woodlands connecting family groups are disappearing and solid walls, roads and railways mean that just getting together for some fun is fraught with danger. Once again, the use of chemicals to improve pasture mean they are deprived of their prey.

We gardeners also have to accept some sort of responsibility when it comes to the decline of hedgehogs. Decking, patios, artificial turf and the desire for neatness in our outside spaces leaves them with nowhere to shelter and little food. They hunt for woodlice, slugs, snails, beetles and bugs, mainly using their sense of smell. They love a windfall apple and really are the gardener's friend, controlling all sorts of garden pests. You scratch their back and they really will – after all they have the tools – scratch yours.

So if you want these prickly chums in the garden, let it all hang out. Leave the leaves, uncover your compost heap, don't use weedkillers or slug pellets, just grab a cup of tea, get comfy and wait for the snuffling to start.

Despite having lived in deepest darkest rural Devon for many years, I have only ever seen one slow worm. It is not a worm nor a snake but is a legless lizard, which means it can shed its tail and blink its eyelids. They are mostly found at woodland edges where they will eat invertebrates while sunning themselves, their beautiful bronze, smooth, burnished skin glowing in the sunlight. In the mating season in May, males become aggressive towards each other. During mating the male takes hold of the female by biting her head or neck. This display can last up to 10 hours, which is frankly ludicrous. You can have too much of a good thing.

Slow worms are protected under the Wildlife and Countryside Act 1991, which means it is an offence to kill, injure or sell them – thank God, because these are the golden thread of our wildlife tapestry and without them our countryside would be hugely diminished.

It's hard for me, as someone who really only knows the natural

world through my time spent in the British countryside and
particularly in my own garden, to have an educated overview of
the situation when it comes to our wildlife and our habitats. My feeling
is, though, that caring for our gardens in a responsible way is a start
and perhaps, just by making small changes and noticing the daily and
seasonal shifts that take place around us, we can be a force for good.

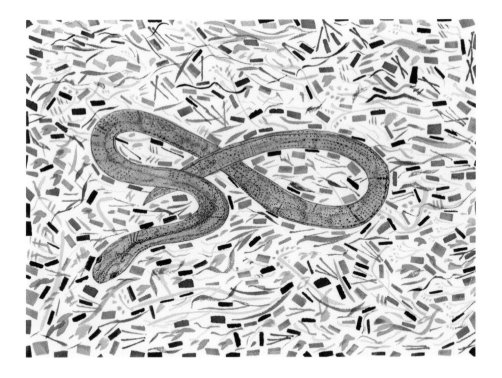

CHAPTER 11

Water

'A pond reflects the sky and
brings it to our feet.'

CAROLINE QUENTIN

When Sam and I moved into this derelict small holding 20 years ago we knew we wanted to encourage wildlife – for us, it was a priority. So we set about creating a pond. The rapid response to the arrival of our pond by ducks, coots and all manner of amphibians was frankly startling. In just two years the pond was established and functioning well. Having never undertaken anything so challenging in my gardening life (previously I'd only had a tiny pond in a London garden – still full of frogs and newts, I'd hasten to add), this was a big step up. It is without doubt the most thrilling gardening adventure of my life.

Water cure

I've met many of you through my Instagram account @cqgardens, and some of you have been lucky enough to see my big, white, wobbly bottom floating in the green chilly waters of our wildlife pond. I make no secret of the fact that swimming is a passion. Whenever I get the chance to get into water – rivers, the sea, lakes, swimming pools, hot tubs or just a good deep bath – I'll grab it with both flippers. So I think it's wonderful that over the last couple of years, wild swimming has gained such momentum and is no longer seen as an unusual pastime but as something that can be enjoyed by lots of us, regardless of our age or gender, and to some extent even our physical abilities. Increasingly, groups of women in particular are taking to bodies of water together for the sake of camaraderie, health and mental wellbeing. I'm not sure of the research exactly but I think there is some evidence to show that a dip in some cold water, as long as you are well prepared and sensible and in company, is good for you. I know that when I'm feeling my age, particularly in my joints and muscles, then just moving my limbs in the water really helps. I'm pretty sure that I've never heard a moorhen complaining of arthritis so I think we are in good company.

The addition of water to any landscape or garden, no matter how big or small, is a catalyst for change on so many levels. A large body of water is, of course, stunningly beautiful. Think of the artificial lakes of garden designers like Capability Brown or the delicate babbling of a stream at the bottom of a cottage garden. Just the addition of a bowl of clean water to a bird-feeding station changes the character of the wildlife interaction. Anyone who has ever seen a baby sparrow mucking about in a couple inches of tap water will tell you it's worth the effort of filling a washing-up bowl. Just a small pond in a suburban back garden can bring dragonflies, frogs, newts and all sorts of hovering, floating, swimming creatures – you may never watch television again. Of course, the benefits of introducing water are primarily to give our wildlife hydration, places to lay their eggs and spawn, make their nests and live their best lives, but once again something we do for them seems to give us equal if not greater benefit.

Bats

As I've said, our house was a small derelict building when we first came. It was a wiggly tin roof held up by six uprights of rotten oak posts housing all manner of creepy crawlies and some seriously unnerving spiders. Before starting work on the house we had a visit from the Bat Conservation Trust because I had spotted some rapid flittering creatures in the twilight and I wanted to make sure Sam and I did nothing to endanger their habitat, their roosts or their way of life. It's worth remembering that it is a criminal offence as well as a moral outrage to take, injure or kill a wild bat or indeed to intentionally disturb a roost. Like most people I find looking into the face of a bat challenging. They are not one of nature's cuddliest or cutest offerings but I would encourage you, however alien it might feel, to overcome any initial repulsion and give it a try.

Of course the likelihood of bumping into a bat is limited. They are shy, rare, silent and intensely private creatures. There are 18 species of bat in the UK – and again, here is the familiar refrain about populations dwindling – but with organisations such as the Bat Conservation Trust, there's hope. One night, almost two years before we moved into our house, I stood on a hill with a man I'd only just met, hearing, with the use of a bat detector (I kid you not – it's a portable echometer, which brings the high-pitched noises bats make down to a frequency that humans can hear), a colony of bats. As the stars came out so did the bats, feeding on the insects floating in the air above the derelict cow shed. I'm delighted to say that 20 years on, and having protected their environment and indeed tried to improve the battiness quotient of our property, we are lucky to briefly see several species of our native bats on a regular basis. I must come clean here though and say that on the few occasions that one mistakenly makes it into the bedroom, I hide under the duvet screaming like a virgin in a Hammer House of Horror film while Sam patiently and calmly removes the mini-Dracula and frees it into the night.

Frogs and toads

Early adopters of the new pond were the frogs and toads – again, not everybody's cup of tea, but stick with me here. Just a little time spent looking at a common frog and I really believe that the beauty of their markings, the golden glow of their skin and their hilarious personality will win you over. Sometimes as early in the year as Valentine's Day, Sam and I are aware of the annual migration of the common frog from its over-wintering sites back to our pond. It's pathetic and so needy of me to feel flattered by this yearly visit. I'm totally aware of the fact that it's the pond they come to see and not me but somehow, isn't it just possible that they miss me over the Christmas holidays? At about three-years-old, the blokes, which have a single vocal sack under their chin, hop on a passing female and grab a lift to the pond – it's impossible to get an Uber out here in the countryside. Clumps of spawn, sometimes huge clouds of it, appear and next, tadpoles (toad tadpoles are black, more of which in a moment). In a few months, tadpoles grow back legs, then front legs and finally leave the water as tiny froglets, as small as a fingernail and heartbreakingly vulnerable.

Having grown up with the film of the Royal Ballet's production of *The Tales of Beatrix Potter* (I was just 11 when it was released), I can't see a frog without thinking of the incredible performance by principal dancer Michael Coleman. Frederick Ashton's choreography was as witty as it was athletic. If you've any ballet-mad kids around it's really worth showing them this film as it still stands up all these years later. Having taken part in *Strictly Come Dancing* and struggled with the sheer weight of sequins and fake tan, the idea of doing a grand jeté with a heavy frog's head blocking my vision and screwing with my balance is mind-boggling. Sorry, back to the pond.

Toads (and if you don't like frogs I have a sense that toads aren't your thing either) are broader, squatter, wartier-skinned and have a John Wayne style of swaggering walk rather than the elegant Nureyev leap of a frog. Most of us meet our first toad in literature, as Mr Toad overturns his horse-drawn caravan when a passing car scares his pony. I've never really understood why Kenneth Graham chose Toad to be such an obsessive, selfish, foolhardy and self-satisfied character. Perhaps it's something to do with their faces. There is a sort of smug and rather immutable quality to their expression. Regardless though, Mr Toad in both Kenneth Graham's book and A.A. Milne's play remains a firm favourite and continues to return to both stage and screen, still delighting generations of children.

Real toads will return to the pond where they were spawned, to mate and continue their life cycle. Laying their eggs a little later than frogs, toad spawn differs from frog spawn in that it is laid in long strips that remind me of cap-gun pellets, for those of you old enough to remember such things. It's really very beautiful. By high summer, usually after a heavy fall of rain, toads will leave the water and spend their winter under compost heaps, secreted in a pile of dead wood and waiting for the spring.

Newts

Having newts in your garden is like having a crack squad of ninjas ready to ambush some of your dreaded enemies. A newt's sticky tongue will

reel in slugs and snails for you but because of a huge decline in numbers you are less likely to see them these days. The UK has three native species: smooth, crested and palmate. These are all the natural predators of frogs, tadpoles and other invertebrates. If you're lucky enough to have newts in your garden, spend a little time watching them move like mini oil slicks in the water.

One winter violent winds sent a piece of rattan furniture flying from the pontoon into the pond. When Sam and I retrieved it in the spring it had become home to over 100 efts, for an eft, I discover, is what a newt calls itself in its juvenile stage. Turning over the bench was such an extraordinary moment as, until we discovered this hoard of little salamanders, we had no idea that the pond was home to such diversity.

Dragonflies

Everybody's got to eat. So who's eating who in your pond? Dragonflies symbolise a self that comes with maturity. They have been a symbol of happiness, new beginnings and change for many centuries and it's easy to see why. With a lifespan of just over a year there are three stages: egg, nymph, adult. Most of the lifecycle is lived in the nymph stage and we will only be lucky enough to see them if we are swimming with our eyes open in a lake or a pond. As adults though, when they are skimming across the water, the sunlight catching the metallic greens, blues and purples of their jewelled bodies, their lacy ethereal wings transporting them from bullrushes to lily pads, we can watch them in wonder.

There are 42 species of resident breeding dragonfly in Britain: 17 damselflies and 25 dragonflies. The most common is the large red damselfly (*Pyrrhosoma nymphula*) and it's the one most of us have spotted at some point. As pond life goes, they are quite low on the food chain because they are predated upon by birds, spiders, frogs and even larger dragonflies. In return though, and I'm always grateful to them for this (particularly around the pond on still summer nights), their diet is, in large part, made up of mosquitoes.

When I was at junior school we did a play about insects. I don't remember how the casting decisions were made but I do recall the fact that a girl called Lucy played a dragonfly. She was costumed in a multitude of shiny, multi-coloured sequins, silks, reflective foil fabrics, translucent and shimmering gossamers and a startling, bejewelled headdress. I was the follow spot operator. The night of the performance it took every ounce of professionalism and concentration my six-year-old body and brain could muster to shine a light on Lucy, an iridescent dragonfly being 'born' in front of an awe-inspired audience, murmuring their approbation and wonderment. I was in the balcony, in the dark and, to all intents and purposes, invisible. 'Where are you now, Lucy?' I often think to myself as I walk out centre stage in the spotlight in the West End, not so shiny now – dragonflies only have a very short lifespan. I do wonder if this wasn't the beginning of my problematic relationship with attention seeking and also my deep-rooted fascination with Odonata/infraorder Anisoptera.

Waterfowl and others

When Sam and I first met we regularly holidayed in a two-up, two-down flint cottage on the north Norfolk coast. We'd head out of London, sometimes getting stuck in traffic for up to six or seven hours, a twelve-year-old collie with dog breath that could strip paint off a Victorian barn door in the boot and an eight-week-old baby in a car seat letting us know that she was pretty miffed at being born ten weeks early. Nonetheless, we arrived in Holme-next-the-Sea tired and hungry and in need of a feed (and I imagine the baby needed something as well), but always with a profound sense of peace. The following morning we'd rise early. For keen birders, water means waterfowl. We would strap our baby daughter to Sam's chest and head out onto the wide, glistening sandbanks of the East Anglian coast. The vastness of the sky, the broad horizons, the rapid changing of the light in this part of the

world, the heartbreaking wistful call of the curlews and sandpipers, seeped into my soul and happily remains an indelible memory. The landscape in south-west England could not be more different from the Norfolk beaches but the lush green hills of home have also proved to be a haven for birdlife. We don't see any waders or huge flocks of pink-footed geese on our bit of land, but by digging a pond we've provided a habitat for so many delightful feathered friends. It's a large stretch of water for a domestic garden, about half an acre, and I've planted it with water lilies, flag irises and water buttercups. Bull rushes have arrived uninvited but now provide a welcome home for coots, dab chicks and moorhens.

Here at the farm our pond has attracted its fair share of wild ducks too. In fact, over the past 20 years all manner of feathered creatures have joined us. Sometimes they stay for a few days, sometimes a few months and, if we're really lucky, some choose to make this place their home. The ducks are pretty much permanent residents now. I'm always surprised at how easy it is to take these extraordinary birds for granted. I suppose we undervalue them because of their association with childhood and municipal ponds and the feeding of breadcrumbs, which, by the way, should only be done in moderation. According to the RSPB it's better to give them sweetcorn, porridge oats, peas and bird seed. However, memories of frosty mornings, handknitted mittens on a string, a runny nose and a paper bag full of stale crusts of bread plus the overwhelming excitement at these wild creatures squabbling and jostling for position to get closer to the bank so that they could enjoy something that we'd bought specially for them from the breakfast table are still with me 60 years later. I wonder if the offspring of the ducks that I fed in Reigate Priory Pond are still there thrilling and terrifying young children as they did in the 1960s.

The electric blue-green of a drake's head shining in the summer sunlight is something that we really should take time to marvel at and, although the hen's plumage is more subtle, when we look closely, its tawny browns and beiges have splashes of religious purple on her wings and eyeliner that would have impressed even the late great Amy Winehouse. Other guests, although it's hard to see them sometimes, include coots and moorhens hiding among the reeds. The sharp electric shock of the 'tak, tak, tak' of an alert mother moorhen makes me jump out of my skin if I disturb her. I'm pretty sure she knows I won't hurt her chicks but then who's to say I'm not acting on behalf of a local dog fox?

The vaguely absurd, wildly head-dressed great crested grebes come to visit sometimes – a pair of spring lovers bobbing their heads up and down, looking towards each other and then away in unison, and then individually, is both ludicrous and heartbreakingly perfect in equal measure. I'm always delighted to see how, when they are only inches away from each other and they whip their head round to look away, only seconds later they are entirely shocked to find their partner is still there, eyebrows raised and waiting for the next bit of the dance.

More secretive, smaller and much harder to spot because of their habit of rapidly dipping under the water, are the other spring visitors; the little grebe or dabchicks (tiny, bobbing, cartoonlike birds whose chicks look like floating false eyelashes). Canada geese visit regularly and never stay. One year a pair of swans arrived, looked like they'd settle but failed to build a nest. Up above the pond, buzzards circle, riding the thermals and keeping their beady eyes open for prey. They will eat frogs, toads, newts, voles, mice and, upsettingly, ducklings and all the other little chicks that they can get their beaks on. The circle of life is sometimes less Disney, more *The Killing Fields*, but there is never a dull moment on the pond.

A pond reflects the sky and brings it to our feet. The supple branches of a willow, dipping into the surface of the water appear infinite. When we glance into a pond we may, like Narcissus, see ourselves gazing back, or we may, if we are lucky, get a glimpse of the heavens that are reflected there.

CHAPTER 12

Scent

'In July when I bury my nose in a hazel-bush,
I feel fifteen years old again. It is good! It smells of love.'

CAMILLE COROT (1796–1875)

More than any other sense, smell transports us to another time, another place. What I always find extraordinary is how almost accidentally a fragrance can bypass the rational part of my brain and with alarming speed teleport me to a feeling, a location, a person and, particularly, to an emotion. The mere suggestion of a perfume on the breeze can take me hostage. As if against my will, it can throw me headlong into feelings of love, loss, desire, fear or excitement. In the garden, I am particularly vulnerable to the assault. Of course, our personal perfume libraries are all stocked with different books. The smell of burnt toast chimes with me because it's the smell of childhood grill pans left unattended in a chaotic family home, but if I had grown up in Rajasthan and not Reigate, the aroma of chai might transport me to a very different childhood breakfast.

A horticultural time capsule

In the garden though, many of us, no matter our life experiences, play out our 'scent movies' as we potter and prune. How does a tomato leaf turn into a time capsule when I crush it in between my fingers? The green stain on my thumb won't last as long as the ache I feel at the sparking of a memory. My son, barely more than a toddler, 'stealing' the low-growing crimson globes and popping them into his mouth, convinced that he was unobserved. He is a grown man now but in the humid heat of a summer greenhouse, I can see him as he was all those years ago by simply squeezing a tomato leaf.

Sometimes a perfume, particularly a floral one, will, as if grabbing me physically around the waist, hurtle me backwards in time, with such startling speed and shocking disregard for my personal agency that I feel as though I have been mugged. Gasping for air, I lift my head to see who would treat me so roughly – the usual suspect is a tea rose. I really think that the Damask roses so popular in my youth are the scent thugs of the garden. I cannot breathe in the scent of an Autumn Damask rose, carried on the air of a warm summer night, and not return to a garden, the long hot summer of 1976 and unrequited teenage love, the lengthening shadows of a majestic cedar tree on the yellowing grass, prickling my bare feet. The object of my passion was a seemingly untraversable three years older than I. If I bury my nose in the musky, heavy, luxury of the petals of an Autumn Damask, I am 16 again. But as I lift my head the scent relinquishes its hold and, like a rose, the ephemeral images fade.

In my own garden, growing plants for their fragrance is something that can be overlooked or come low on my list of priorities, but as I get older, I find it more and more important. While I love the robust joy of pulling up a carrot (and carrots really do smell divine when they are first drawn out of the earth), the honeysuckle that envelops the wall by the path to the greenhouse has a pervasive, lasting, weighty cloak of scent. Lavender, in full flower on a hot summer's day, can almost drown me in a scent that won't allow me to remain in the present day but insists on dragging me back to sewing lessons and the lavender bags we all seemed to make in the 1960s. Lavender was the floral scent of British knickers for the best part of a hundred years. Everyone had a little cotton bag, stuffed with the dried flower heads and tied with a ribbon, tucked into their underwear drawers.

Lavender was the floral scent of British knickers for the best part of a hundred years.

Good scents

I love the fact that some perfumes are beautiful to some and totally objectionable to others. I adore the smell of the wormwood (*Artemisia absinthium*). If you don't know it, it's a herbaceous perennial, silvery white, growing to about 1.5 m (5 ft) in height. The leaves are silky white on the underside and have tiny oil-producing glands. It's a fantastic 'filler', especially in a border that needs paler backdrop planting.

Wormwood is mentioned in Shakespeare – it's known for its antibacterial properties and is used for flavouring drinks, works as a flea repellent and is thought to have many uses as a herbal medicine, but it is the scent that fascinates me and keeps me coming back. The perfume industry uses it, primarily in scents aimed at the male market, and the fragrance is known as 'bitter' and 'green'. This doesn't really do it justice, though. I think the smell of wormwood is a mix of smoke, incense and cut grass. It is both known and foreign and, I know this will sound odd, but if I come across wormwood on a warm summer night, it's the closest I ever get to believing in ghosts. I always have the sense that there is an unseen gardener from a bygone era standing near me, perhaps a cloth-capped under-gardener from a grand Victorian walled garden, or Gertrude Jekyll slowly perambulating the beds. They are breathing on my neck and encouraging me to tend the plants and keep the garden in good shape (I told you it would sound odd).

Some of my other favourite scented plants have less-complicated perfumes. I'm often contacted by folk when I mention that my love of sweet peas is linked, inextricably, with memories of my mother and her memories of her mother. They were her favourite, too.

Do you know the painting *Carnation, Lily, Lily, Rose* by John Singer Sargent? It's a personal favourite. It's the sublime depiction of two little girls holding paper lanterns in a lushly planted garden on a summer evening. Painted in 1885/6, the girls are peering into the lit lanterns in the twilight. Amid carnations and pinks, they are surrounded by white lilies that reach way over their heads. When I see the painting I can almost smell the intoxicating scent of the white oriental lilies, their petals bent back, the pollen-laden stamen heavy in the blooms, which are at the peak of perfection. I believe it's as close as a picture can get to producing a scent memory. I know for some people the smell of lilies has connotations of grief and loss, and for others, memories of weddings. In the garden, though, I think they are released from the firm tether of association to occasion. I think a big pot of lilies is always bliss, visually, but particularly for their scent (and they do so well in pots). A few bulbs in a well-drained container, planted in early autumn, will produce a fabulous summer display. There are so many colours to choose from, from hot pinks and reds to strong oranges and yellows, pale apricots and pure glacial whites. There are trumpet lilies and oriental and Asiatic hybrids (though the Asiatic tend to be unscented). For planting in containers, I stick to the shorter types as they are less likely to need support.

Plant in large pots, using multipurpose compost, and keep them well fed and watered (I use a liquid tomato feed). If you refresh the top layer of compost, they will perform again the following year, but you might need to wrap the pot to protect them against the coldest weather.

Be warned though, that turning a corner and bumping into a cloud of scent from a pot full of lilies in full bloom may leave you incapable of speech for several hours. It's like being a child clutched to the bosom of a big-breasted maiden aunt at the end of a boozy Christmas party. She won't let go until you are quite faint, gasping for air, intoxicated from the mere proximity of her.

Smell the roses

On the dresser in my kitchen I have three dried roses. They are faded and wrinkled and it's hard to distinguish their original colours but they still each of them retain a very delicate scent, or at least I believe they do. I wonder sometimes if my mind supplies a perfume that is, in reality, no longer there.

They each come from the funeral flowers of women I have loved. The pale cream one is from the flowers that were on my best friend's coffin. The white one from my sister-in-law's willow casket. The last, a pale pink, is from the wreath on my mother's grave.

I know these dried flowers might seem sentimental and maudlin to some, but I genuinely don't find them so. Rather, they act a as a reminder to me to live in the present, to sow seeds, grow flowers, plant trees and at the very least … to *always* make time to stop and smell the roses, while we can.

Epilogue

When the going gets tough . . . the tough get growing!
 Like many of us, as a child I often felt frightened and alone. Even as adults the world can be a daunting place – and whether we are nine or ninety, many of us can feel lonely, scared or overwhelmed.

Nature and gardening bring me peace of mind and a sense of constancy in an unpredictable life.

We gardeners are optimists. To sow a seed is an act of hope, and to plant a tree is to believe in the future. Even in the short, cold days of winter, gardeners know that the warmth of spring is just around the corner.

I hope you have enjoyed this book. If you don't yet grow things, perhaps you will start. If you've always wanted to draw or paint but haven't had the confidence, maybe now you'll give it a try?

If you need me, you know where I'll be. Trowel in hand and watering can at the ready, looking forward to whatever comes up!

INDEX

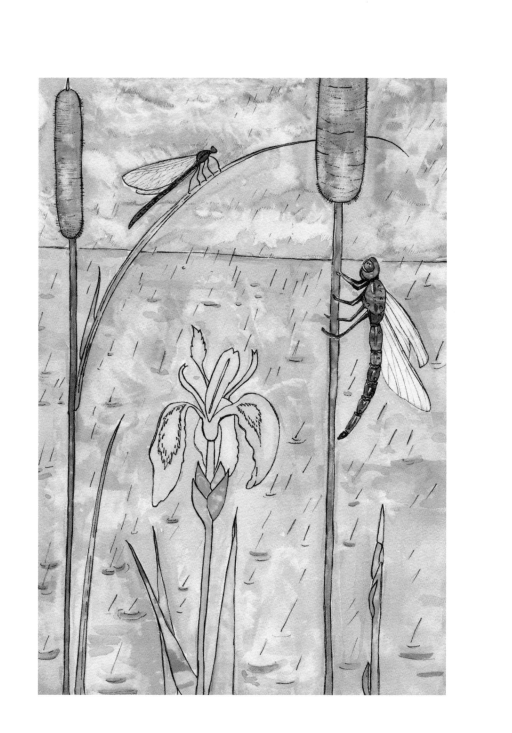

Thanks to Anthony Adams, whose hard work and can-do spirit helped me make my dream garden a reality.

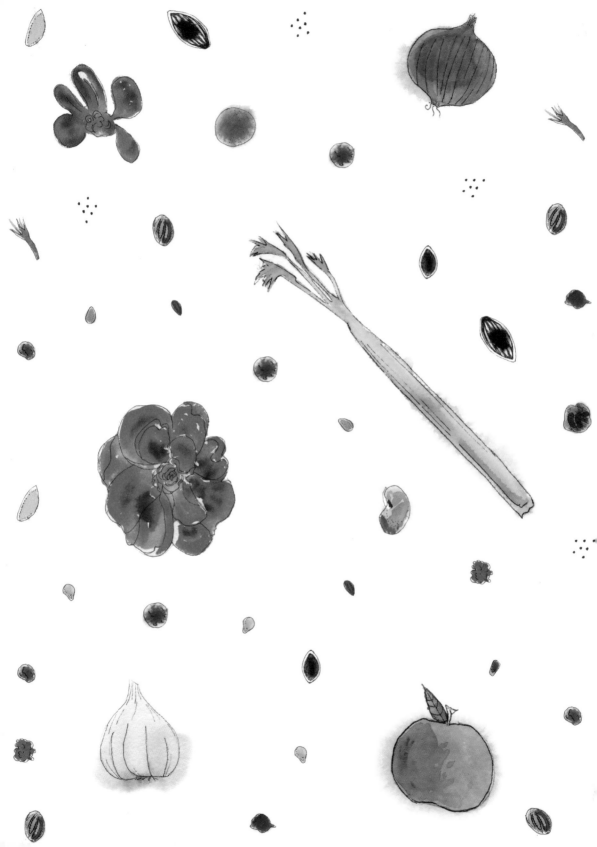